Studies in African American History and Culture

Edited by
Graham Russell Hodges
Colgate University

A Routledge Series

Studies in African American History and Culture

Graham Russell Hodges, *General Editor*

Africans and Indians
An Afrocentric Analysis of Contacts Between Africans and Indians in Colonial Virginia
Barbara A. Faggins

New York's Black Regiments During the Civil War
William Seraile

Jesuit Slaveholding in Maryland, 1717–1838
Thomas Murphy, S.J.

"White" Americans in "Black" Africa
Black and White American Methodist Missionaries in Liberia, 1820–1875
Eunjin Park

The Origins of the African American Civil Rights Movement, 1865–1956
Aimin Zhang

Religiosity, Cosmology, and Folklore
The African Influence in the Novels of Toni Morrison
Therese E. Higgins

Something Better for Our Children
Black Organizing in Chicago Public Schools, 1963–1971
Dionne Danns

Teach the Nation
Public School, Racial Uplift, and Women's Writing in the 1890s
Anne-Elizabeth Murdy

The Art of the Black Essay
From Meditation to Transcendence
Cheryl B. Butler

Emerging Afrikan Survivals
An Afrocentric Critical Theory
Kamau Kemayó

Slavery in the Cherokee Nation
The Keetoowah Society and the Defining of a People, 1855–1867
Patrick N. Minges

Troubling Beginnings
Trans(per)forming African American History and Identity
Maurice E. Stevens

The Social Teachings of the Progressive National Baptist Convention, Inc., Since 1961
A Critical Analysis of the Least, the Lost, and the Left-out
Albert A. Avant, Jr.

Giving a Voice to the Voiceless
Four Pioneering Black Women Journalists
Jinx Coleman Broussard

Constructing Belonging
Class, Race, and Harlem's Professional Workers
Sabiyha Prince

Contesting the Terrain of the Ivory Tower

Spiritual Leadership of African-American Women in the Academy

Rochelle Garner

NEW YORK AND LONDON

Published in 2004 by
Routledge
711 Third Avenue, New York, NY 10017

Published in Great Britain by
Routledge
2 Park Square, Milton Park, Abingdon, Oxfordshire OX14 4RN

Routledge is an imprint of the Taylor & Francis Group

Transferred to Digital Printing 2005

First issued in paperback 2012

10 9 8 7 6 5 4 3 2 1

Library of Congress Cataloging-in-Publication Data

Garner, Rochelle.
Contesting the terrain of the ivory tower : spiritual leadership of African-American women in the academy / Rochelle Garner.
p. cm. — (Studies in African American history and culture)
Includes bibliographical references and index.
ISBN 0-415-94798-7 (Hardcover : alk. paper)
1. African American women college administrators—Case studies. 2. Educational leadership—Case studies. 3. Spiritual life—Case studies. I. Title. II. Series: Studies in African American history and culture.
LB2341.G29 2003
2003015083

ISBN 13: 978-0-415-94798-5 (hbk)
ISBN 13: 978-0-415-64698-7 (pbk)

Dedication

To my Ancestral Spirit: my late grandmother, Lydia Alline Smith Hayden, for inspiring me to develop a thirst for education. For the foundation and love you gave me, it's all because of you that I am Who I am, and Whose I am.

To the Spirit that lives: my son, Jerusa Amar Garner-Simmons, for inspiring me to push beyond boundaries as a parent and African-American woman. Your energy and six-year-old wisdom brings me great joy and inspiration to be the "bestest" mom for you. Thank you for the many teaching/learning moments we have shared together. You are truly a blessing from God. Because of you, I am Who I am.

Contents

ACKNOWLEDGMENTS ix

SETTING THE CONTEXT xi

CHAPTER 1
When and Where We Enter the Academy: Telling (Her)Story 3
- Research Purpose 4
- Definition of Spirituality 4
- Socio-Historical Framework of African-American Women 5
- Empowering Resistance in the Academy 8
- Stony the Road We Trod: A Brief History of Higher Education for African Americans and the Experiences of African-American Women 10
- We'll Let Nobody Turn Us around: Three Women Exemplars from Our Past 12
- Looking toward the Future 21

CHAPTER 2
Surveying the Literature 23
- Leadership Theory 25
- Feminist/Womanist Theory 28
- Spiritual Theories 31

CHAPTER 3
Methodology 37
- Data and Analysis 42
- Selection of Participants 43

Interview Process 43
Research Design 44
Analysis 45

CHAPTER 4
Flat-Footed Truths: Telling Black Women's Lives 47
Adjuoa 48
Jewel 52
Chaka 57

CHAPTER 5
The Soul of My Sisters: Talkin' and Testifyin' 63
Theme One: Spiritually Guided Leadership through Servanthood 64
Theme Two: A Call to Consciousness in Everyday Practice: Exercising an Ethic of Care 67
Theme Three: Spiritually Guided Leadership for Social Justice 72
Theme Four: Leading beyond the Borders of Academe 76

CHAPTER 6
Still Lifting as We Climb 79
Theme One: Spiritually Guided Leadership through Servanthood 80
Theme Two: A Call to Consciousness in Everyday Practice: Exercising an Ethic of Care 82
Theme Three: Spiritually Guided Leadership for Social Justice 87
Theme Four: Leading beyond the Borders of Academe 90
Summary 92

CHAPTER 7
Our Spiritual Strivings 95

APPENDIX A: LETTER 103

NOTES 107

BIBLIOGRAPHY 117

INDEX 123

Acknowledgments

FIRST, I GIVE THANKS AND HONOR TO GOD FOR GIVING ME THE STRENGTH, courage, and wisdom to endure this journey. It is all because of you that I live, Lord. Only you know the trials and tribulations I have encountered personally, physically, and academically. I know that it was only your "Footprints" that carried me throughout this journey.

I would like to thank the wonderful women in this study for being patient with me, and allowing me the opportunity to enter into their lives. Thank you for your words of wisdom and encouragement throughout this process.

Then, to the wonderful women on my dissertation committee, I know that the way we came together was a gift from God. I am forever grateful for your words of encouragement, guidance, and support throughout my educational experience at Miami University. Clearly, my research could not have been done without your guidance. Sally, your willingness to allow your office to become "my" office has been a blessing. Judy, our lunch meetings and girlfriend chats have also been a blessing, especially in an environment that sometimes had a tendency to become quite chilly. Kathy, your encouragement and pushing me to think about my research will never be forgotten. Susan, our "kindred spirits" have been more than a blessing since the day we talked about working together in the Dean's office. Thanks for your words of encouragement, mentoring, and pushing me beyond the boundaries to develop my own teaching and research interests. Finally, Dr. Michael Dantley (my honorary committee member), I am forever grateful for taking the extra time to work with me on my research, and pushing me to the finish line.

Many people, family, friends, and acquaintances have assisted me and offered words of encouragement and prayers along the way. I want to especially thank the Brown family for their unconditional love, care, and support for (adopting my family) walking with me and encouraging me every step of the way. You truly have been a blessing to me! Thank you so much Mother Brown for inspiring me to be "bold and courageous!"

I want to thank the Gillespies', the Leonards', and the Miringus' for your care and support in helping me with Jerusa while I was completing my research. I am forever grateful.

Beatrice was always there with a cup of Kenyan tea whenever I needed to take a break or just come together and talk about whatever was on my mind. Thanks for listening. You are a wonderful woman, and I know our spirits will connect wherever we are in the world. Thanks for your words of wisdom, support, and most of all being a "real" sistah friend. My sister, Ramona, sent me tons of e-mails with words of inspiration. I truly appreciate your words of encouragement and prayers throughout this journey. Even when things got tough, you brought me back to life with a good laugh. Laughter creates smiles, and smiles warm the heart . . . thanks so much for your love and care. My sister friend Karen Byrd, a true prayer warrior, always offered words of encouragement and "kept me lifted up!" Thanks so much for your love and sisterhood. Dianne and Dorothy, thanks for your support from the beginning to the end. I truly appreciate our many conversations and sisterhood we have shared along the way. Denise and I worked together as research buddies. We met regularly to discuss our research, set goals, and kept each other focused on our work. Your friendship and support goes unmeasured. I am glad our Women's Studies course brought us together four years ago. Denise, Regina, and Selena allowed me to "break loose" and let my drama flow whenever I needed to talk and have a listening ear. Thanks for allowing me to have one of those "front row" seats in your lives.

Finally, I must thank my friends and extended family in Lexington, Kentucky, and on the East Coast. Thanks for your cards, phone calls, and e-mails encouraging me to keep my eyes on the prize!

Setting the Context

WHEN I FIRST BEGAN THIS DOCTORAL PROGRAM SEVERAL YEARS AGO, I honestly had no idea where I would end up in terms of my research and career interests. Since I worked in Student Affairs prior to this program, I thought it would be plausible to explore African-American women's leadership, knowing that I had intentions to return to Student Affairs with leadership as a focus. After arriving at Miami University and encountering some "strange happenings," it became evident to me that I needed to recover my voice, which had suddenly become dormant at this majority institution; especially since I had recently left a Historically Black College and University (HBCU) on the East Coast. For example, when I applied to the doctoral program at Miami, after the interview, I walked away feeling that more concern or emphasis had been placed on my spouse's educational and career interests. Because of the type of questions asked, I left thinking, "these people think that I just need something to do with my time until my spouse finishes his program." Never had I felt more invisible than at that moment, feeling as if people saw me standing in the shadow of someone else. It's not as if I've lived my life in a bubble depending upon a man or someone else to take care of my every need.

The foundation of my educational experience was influenced by my grandmother, who always impressed upon me that the most important thing that I could do in life was to get a good education. Second, throughout my post-secondary education I have chosen on my own terms whether or not to pursue advanced degrees. Throughout my life, I have stood my own ground; therefore standing in the shadow of another has been quite the opposite of my experience. Furthermore, my life's foundational and educational experiences taught me to stand on the frontline, addressing issues of social justice whenever I have been in a position to do so.

The interview experience, nevertheless, reminded me just how much women are still seen as second-class citizens in many arenas, and the Academy carries as much guilt as any other organization. Clearly, gender issues were pronounced on both campuses I have attended, the HBCU and the majority institution. While the small size of the HBCU made for a more intimate climate, one could encounter friendly faces saying "hello" regardless of one's race or gender. Issues of race became more apparent to me while matriculating at this majority institution, even though cultural diversity was the buzzword around campus.

Though I had grown up in Lexington, Kentucky, a predominantly Euro-American city located two hours south of Oxford, and had attended schools with affluent students like those at Miami University, I was quite naïve when I moved, thinking that any state north of Kentucky had made substantial progress in dealing with racial issues and people of different ethnic groups. Much to my surprise and dismay, I was totally wrong. To say the least, the cultural shock set in and I dealt with the reality of the striking differences among these institutions. In order to make sense of my earlier experiences at Miami University, I reflected upon my past, trying to make sense of the cultural environment with which I found myself. This cultural switch forced me to continue to draw upon my spirituality, which has served as the sustaining force in my life. More importantly for my own sense of being, I became interested in learning more about African-American women's leadership and how these women navigated their way through places and spaces like Miami University, a place that often times felt isolating and secluded.

During my first year here, I wisely took the advice of one of my professors and decided to be open about my research, by not couching things in a fixed mode and being open to examining my research interest from various perspectives. In doing so, I found a void in the literature on how African-American women use their spirituality in their leadership, though I had not originally considered this a part of my study. To be honest, the "Aha" moment arrived while taking a course on *Transformative Leadership,* where we read works by Parker Palmer and Robert J. Starratt. These readings caused me to reflect on other research I had conducted on the lives of African and African-American women, and how they mentioned their spiritual life as being a part of who they are and the one of the things that are important to them. In turn, I began to think about how these women's spirituality manifested itself in their everyday leadership practices.

For the most part, that's where my journey began, and that's how I arrived at where I am today. Conducting several qualitative studies on African-American women's leadership in higher education led me to probe further ideas that were mentioned on spirituality, but not fully explicated. For example, in one of the qualitative studies, I interviewed African-

American women focusing on their career development. One common theme for these women was their involvement in their community and church. They also acknowledged their belief in a higher power greater than themselves, and how their faith has helped them to sustain their belief that they could and would be successful in whatever role they were "called" to do. Many of these women looked at their work as service, working with and helping others in their day-to-day experiences was very meaningful to them. Much of what was being shared coincided with my research on African-American women's feminist and womanist literature.

As I further explored this topic on leadership, some of the same ideas were confirmed in a different qualitative study with women I interviewed in Ghana, West Africa, during the summer of 1998. The Ghanaian women once again expressed their need to create agency for others, and in the process it was empowering for them to serve in roles where a woman had never served. For instance, one woman was the first to serve as the Vice President for Academic Affairs at the University of Ghana, while another woman was the first woman to serve as the Director for Continuing Education at this same university. These women confessed that their faith, belief in themselves, and hard work were determining factors in their success.

Finally, I decided to conduct a pilot focus group on African-American women's spirituality and leadership, and found the responses to the questions raised quite compelling in regard to the spiritual nature of the participants' lives, and what I had already begun to hypothesize. For this study, however, I chose not to use a focus group because I learned in the pilot study that individual interviews would allow the participants more time to give voice to their own personal perspectives, which provided greater depth and offered a better understanding of their leadership experience.

These studies were not the only precursors for this research project, but the literature review conducted also supported many of my ideas, while at the same time it confirmed that there is a void in the literature on African-American women's spiritual leadership in higher education. These studies and the research continues to confirm that, "Yes, we are a spiritual people," but then the question I raised was "What is it that is not being said that could make my research more meaningful as I talk about African-American women's leadership in the Academy?" The answer became quite clear to me: I needed to learn how these women's spirituality manifested itself in their everyday leadership practice and how it could serve in a transformative way to help create change in higher education.

In this case study, three African-American women deans have shared their lives with me to talk about their spirituality and leadership. All women are from majority institutions. Interestingly, none of the women mapped out the deanship in their career path, but all were identified by others to take on the challenge. As you will see in this study, these women's spirituality and leadership is inextricably woven together by the way in which they talk about their lives, relationships, and leadership practices.

Unquestionably, I must take a look at my own situated identity because as a researcher "disinterestedness" would not serve this study well. In spite of my acceptance of this scholarly role and responsibility as a researcher, I cannot, nor do I want to, set aside the fact that the story of these African-American women and how spirituality is interwoven into their leadership is my story too. Clearly, I will place myself in this process by connecting myself to the stories being told by the women in this study. Throughout this work I will use the pronoun "we" and quite clearly signal that this "we" extends beyond the women in this study, including myself and other African-American women. In other words, the shift in viewpoint will occur deliberately, and consciously. Therefore, I clearly intend for myself to be viewed as one among those who constitute this discourse.

In light of all that has been said, I must first acknowledge my own sense of spiritual awareness, which has been influenced by my upbringing and the institution of a church. Yet, my spiritual self is not predicated on religious dogma, but by the way I see the world and how I encounter it on a day-to-day basis in the spiritual realm. Recognizing that there is a power greater than myself is first and foremost. Being open to the process of self-reflection and making the deep changes that need to occur for me to have positive experiences with other human beings by treating people as I would want to be treated, and having empathy for the disenfranchised, are all characteristics which describe my own spiritual process. When I reflect on the influence of my grandmother, I have to acknowledge her impact and how she has molded my life in a very important way. These ideas were articulated at a Women's Celebration where I was asked to give a testimonial on an experience or the impact of another individual on my life, and here is what I revealed, which gives the reader and those who listened at the program an upfront and personal glimpse of who I am. This is the message I shared on March 2, 2001:

"MY SOUL LOOKS BACK AND WONDERS HOW I GOT OVER"

Good Afternoon, I bring you greetings in the spirit of my ancestors who have gone before. I am Rochelle, the daughter of Billie, the daughter of Lydia, the daughter of Amy; and I am also the daughter of many Othermothers, even one of our Honoree's today. (PAUSE)

My Soul Looks Back and Wonders How I Got Over . . . First, I must give thanks and honor to God for being here today. The Soul force of my life from where I draw upon my strength and help through whatever situation I may be going through. Then, I want to pay special homage to my late grandmother, Lydia Alline, who I used to call "Momma." My grandmother was my Harriet Tubman, Sojourner Truth, and Fannie Lou Hamer all in one. My grandmother was the most important role model in my life. It was my grandmother who taught me at a young age to develop a strong belief system and reverence for God. It was my grandmother who helped me to develop a strong sense of self. To believe in myself and love myself for who I am not based on anyone else's terms but my own.

You see, my grandmother was a drum major for social justice and she taught me at a very young age to understand what racism and prejudice was about in this country. This became more apparent when I was in the first grade and a child called me a name that I wasn't familiar with, but I knew it was wrong. When I went home and told my grandmother, she explained to me that I let no one, under any circumstances, call me a name other than Rochelle. My grandmother taught me that I was a special child of God. She taught me that all people were special in the eyes of God despite the fact that there were [and still are] some very mean people in this world. So, when my soul looks back and wonders how I got to where I am today after losing both of my parents by the age of 16, I know it was my faith and a grandmother who was there for me.

My grandmother taught me about the social and political structure of our country. She was the one who taught me about Civil Rights, Women's Rights and why it was important to vote. She taught me the importance of standing up for myself and standing for what is right. It was my grandmother who taught me about the importance of serving my community. It was my grandmother who instilled within me that one of the most important things that I could do in life was to get the best education possible, and acquire all that I could in the process. It was my grandmother who instilled within me the desire to be the best that I possibly could be. It was my grandmother who didn't really want me to get married, but focused me more on education and my becoming independent enough to take care of myself regardless of life's circumstances and situations. Yes, she was the one who took great PRIDE in telling young men in high school who would come to visit me upon occasions (that's when she would let them in the door) . . . "Rochelle has never had to cook" hoping to scare them away, [and, I'm serious!] but also leaving on their minds the notion not to think about anything serious with her granddaughter. Then, she would walk away snickering while I would have to bite my tongue and later tell her not to say such things. But of course, she would look at me and laugh again. So you know, when my soul looks back and wonders how I got over, I know it was because of this strong, independent, and spiritual woman who taught me much of what I know, and I am truly grateful.

Even today, as I continue to deal with life's challenges on a day-to-day basis . . . it's my faith that carries me through it all, and I continue to reflect on the words of my grandmother, "Honey, if there is a Will there is a Way," and, "Child, the Lord will not put any more on you than what you can bear." Though there are days when I want to say "Momma, when can I stop bearing this challenge or that challenge," but I keep on because my SOUL keeps telling me to stay in the "faith zone," and the words resonate . . . that "the race is not given to the swift, nor to the strong, but to them who endureth to the end . . . "[1] *As I continue to move forward in this life, I know that it's God's grace, my faith and belief in myself that continues to carry me.*

For those of you who have been confronted with situations or circumstances beyond your control . . . I leave you with this message of hope: don't give up no matter what you're going through, and allow your faith and belief in yourself to achieve great things. It's your faith that will carry you through the storm when all else seems to fail; it's your faith that will guide you and show you your rightful place here on earth where only you can serve. Because it's only your footprints and handprints that were designed to do whatever it is you've been called to do. So, if you haven't discovered your purpose in life . . . then bear more on your faith and seek guidance from the Source, and I'm certain you'll find your rightful place and better understand your "calling." Then, when your soul looks back and wonders . . . you'll know how you got over!
PEACE and BLESSINGS EVERYONE

After this presentation, I had a number of African-American women students share with me how much my testimony was reminiscent of their own experiences with either their grandmother or other relatives. In this respect, "A people's ethos is the tone, character, and quality of their life, its moral and aesthetic style and mood; it is the underlying attitude toward themselves and their world that life reflects."[2] The story-telling is reflective of the cultural nuances of the African-American experience, which extends throughout the diaspora among people of African descent.

During this seven-minute presentation, I could hear recitations from the audience as I said certain lines that were familiar to many African Americans. Culturally, this familiarity and "call-response" reflects the handing down of spiritual values and lessons conveyed in the African-American community. It was not surprising when I looked into the audience and saw the guest speaker, Alelia Bundles, sitting before me reciting these phrases with the audience.

Later that afternoon, when I returned to the Educational Leadership Department, I had one of my professors share with me how the audience at her table engaged in my presentation through a form of "call-response." Though this European-American professor, whom I highly respect, could not articulate the "strange" happening as "call-response," she knew something was taking place that was endemic to African-American culture because of what she witnessed of the people around her. This phenomenon is clearly a part of the oral tradition in African-American culture as Geneva Smitherman (1977) defines it in her work *Talkin and Testifyin: The Language of Black America.*[3]

Naturally, the very message recited to others continues to ring in my ears today because it's out of my own past and present experience, which causes me to draw upon my spirituality. By far, this doctoral journey has not been easy. Being married with a son has been a challenge in and of itself, though I think that I have adapted well at attempting to balance these various responsibilities. However, it has not always felt good knowing that for more than half of my son's life I have been a student. These last two years have been even more of a challenge while taking on the role of being a single parent while my spouse worked abroad. Admittedly, these last two years have required me to sacrifice my academic work to some degree because of my need to focus on the gift of taking care of the son I was blessed with seven years ago. Clearly, my faith, perseverance and determination has kept me from giving up; especially, since there is quite a bit of research that shows African-American women are the largest population who do not complete their terminal degrees.

Well, I am determined to defy the odds for several reasons. First, I have never given up on my education and cannot allow myself to do so now. Secondly, I would not be at peace with myself if I were to do so. Thirdly, I realize that in order to make a real career in Academia I must have my doctorate. So, as the song goes by the musical artist McFadden and Whitehead, "Ain't no stopping [me] now!"[4] My spiritual roots call out to me in the words of my grandmother, "Getting an education is something that no one can take away from you." Throughout my entire life of knowing my grandmother, she repeated those words to me, continuously reemphasizing the importance of an education. Pursuing this degree, thus, is not just for me, but for my son and my late grandmother.

Since I have yet to travel the road of leadership to the extent of the women in this study, I am truly grateful to the foremothers and the contemporary women for sharing their lives with me. In this case study, the reader will learn that these women's stories is only a glimpse into the window of their lives since time does not permit me to create a biography of the full essence of who they are. Yet, I am certain one will be able to ascertain the rich spirit that lives within these women. Consequently, I openly and proudly acknowledge my identity within this story. I believe that my personal passion, as it comes forth in its openness, does not for one moment change one iota the realities of these women's lives.

Ultimately, I want to talk about these women's lives in the "right now," as I have offered the stories of the foremothers who have gone before us. I want our ways of knowing and being to be acknowledged and recognized today through the discourse of spirituality and leadership while these women are still with us on the planet in mind, body, and spirit. Rightfully so, our story must be told since the true essence of African-American culture embodies a spiritual dynamism which has served as the sustaining force despite the social, historical and political nature of our lives in this country. As Jacqueline Jones Royster (2000) talks about African-American women in *Traces of a Stream*, I too contend that in the context of a nation where race, class, gender, and culture matter, the women in this particular study have been not only innovative but also bold and courageous. I am pleased to pay tribute and let their lives speak.

The first chapter provides the basis for this work, a brief history of African-Americans' educational and cultural experience pre- and post-slavery, along with sharing the lives of three African-American women who were considered the "race" women and trailblazers of their time in higher education.

The second chapter provides a theoretical discussion that requires the blending of three particular theoretical discourses to fully explicate the characterization of African-American women's leadership experiences in higher education. Three particular discourses that have been woven together are feminist/womanist theory, leadership theory, and spiritual theory. All three theories are embedded within a cultural framework.

The third chapter focuses on the research methodology and methods. While the former focuses on the overarching theoretical framework that informs this research, the latter will explicate the ways in which this research has been carried out.

The fourth chapter introduces the three women deans in this study, providing a biographical sketch of their lives. The fifth chapter then offers concrete narratives identified by the emerging themes that unfolded.

The sixth chapter integrates these women's narratives with theories to help inform the way they have talked about their leadership and spirituality, and how these dimensions are holistically bound in the way they live and lead their lives. In essence, the dimension of the spiritual being cannot be separated from the whole of these women's lives and the work they do. Finally, the seventh chapter focuses on the summary and conclusion raising critical questions about leadership in the Academy.

Contesting the Terrain of the Ivory Tower

Chapter 1
When and Where We Enter the Academy: Telling (Her)Story

> When and where I enter, in the quiet, undisputed dignity of my womanhood, without violence and without suing, or special patronage, then and there the whole Negro race enters with me. —Anna Julia Cooper

HISTORICALLY, THE AFRICAN-AMERICAN WOMAN HAS ADAPTED TO A position of marginality in American culture since the inception of Slavery upon these North Atlantic shores. Inasmuch as this may be the case, African-American women have found ways to sustain themselves in every aspect of society as a means to withstand the triple oppressions of race, class, and gender. One formidable way in which Black women have resisted against such ills has been through their own source of spirituality. Quite clearly, this spirituality has served as a practice of freedom despite the multitude of challenges they have endured. Hence, this spirituality derives from an African/African-American ontology. In essence, this spirituality is a powerful and empowering process—one that involves African Americans with a liberating encounter, liberating reflection, and a liberating action,[1] which can be seen in the lives of the women in this study. Although scholars have brought forth some research on the subject of African-American women's leadership, not enough has been written about the various ways in which they lead, especially when examining the intersection of spirituality and leadership. By not telling our own stories, it would leave us ". . . detached from our feelings, our voice, our intelligence, [and cut off], which in turn leaves scars—scars we have hidden too long and for which we are paying a great price. Telling our own stories . . . can heal those scars and leave us more whole."[2]

Recognizably, the subject of spirituality conjures up various notions and ideas for different groups of people, depending upon who is engaging in the discourse at hand. Interestingly enough, spirituality has become a hot topic in today's pop culture and the many circles of medicine, business and education, just to name a few. Spirituality has become a commodity in and of itself; it's been marketed, packaged and sold, dressed up and redefined depending upon its audience. Admittedly, thanks to Oprah Winfrey, Iyanla Vanzant, Deepak Chopra and others, it is now okay to talk about spirituality in just about any circle we can imagine. Thus, this new thing we're talking about unequivocally is not so new, especially, among people of African descent in America. From a socio-historical perspective, spirituality has been the sustaining force in the African-American community, which has given us hope despite the challenges we have had to endure in these United States of America.

RESEARCH PURPOSE

The purpose of this study is to examine the ways in which African-American women make meaning of their spiritual selves in their everyday leadership practices. How does it influence their work and the type of relationships with others in the Academy? Again, I pose the question in a different way: how is African-American women's spirituality interwoven in their day-to-day leadership practices, and how do they make meaning of their lived experience in the Academy? What are the ways in which African-American women have used their spirituality as a lens to lead, and how does this leadership impact the social, cultural, and political construct of a male-dominated arena?

DEFINITION OF SPIRITUALITY

On the one hand, I realize that for some academicians, the topic of spirituality can be frightening, especially if it conjures up notions of religious dogma, mythology, and superstition. On the other hand, talking about spirituality can serve to be enlightening and encouraging for others who are interested in learning more about spiritual leadership and transforming the Academy. However, I am not interested in making sense of religious dogma.

Similar to Astin and Astin (1999), I am using spirituality in the sense of understanding the women's " . . . sense of self, sense of mission and purpose in life, and the personal meaning that one makes out of one's work,"[3] and one's belief in a higher power greater than one's self. In addition, I am attempting to understand and describe the five tenets of African American spirituality as identified by Carlyle Fielding Stewart (1999) in *Black Spirituality and Black Consciousness*, which " . . . issue from the divine soul center as a practice of human freedom an ethos that is formative, unitive or integrative, corroborative, transformative, and sacralative or consecrative."[4] Thus, African-American spirituality is a creative process and practice by which Black people interpret, respond to, shape, and live out their understandings of divine reality and culture in the context of racial, political, and social oppression and life in general. African-American spirituality helps to create mechanisms of Black culture, community, and consciousness.[5]

Finally, spirituality is not a "warm and fuzzy" kind of experience, as some people in Academia may claim. Derived from an African-American cultural ethos, "spirituality involves the whole person, within the whole community of faith, with the whole of life."[6] Furthermore, an African-American ethos departs from modernistic trappings of dualistic notions: body and soul, inhabitants of heaven and earth, separated by good and evil. An African-American ethos embodies a spirit of holism as noted by Michael Dash, Jonathan Jackson, and Stephen Rasor (1997), when they offer, "We are whole people, experiencing all of life, in the whole of existence. Our spirituality reinforces a connectedness that integrates the totality of existence."[7]

SOCIO-HISTORICAL FRAMEWORK OF AFRICAN-AMERICAN WOMEN

In contextualizing the lives of African-American women, I would be remiss not to offer a historical backdrop of who we are and our evolvement in this country. As previously stated, African-American women have had to adapt to a position of marginality in American culture since the inception of slavery. Yet, African-American women have found ways to sustain themselves in every aspect of society as a means to withstand the triple oppressions of race, class, and gender. Spirituality has served as one source for African-American women to resist various oppressive structures in our society.

Manning Marable and Leith Mullings (2000) note that throughout the African-American experience, spirituality has been a source for human renewal, survival, and resistance. The meaning of faith in the Black mind in slavery was a rock upon which the oppressed could find human dignity and hope for the future.[8] Despite every form of institutional oppression, slaves were able to create another world, a counterculture within the Eurocentric-defined world, complete with their own spirituals, folklore and religious practices.[9]

From slavery to freedom, African peoples brought with them a message of hope—their spirituality. Such messages were communicated through spirituals, as they sang of freedom and hope to survive. A number of spirituals were protest songs used to announce secret meetings, planned escapes, and the route and risk of the freedom trail. Manning and Mullings

(2000) also acknowledge this counter-discourse, and state that many historians have observed that the same spirituals contained hidden messages that could serve as coded language, communicating information among slaves without the knowledge of overseers and masters. The themes of suffering and struggle, faith and transcendence, are all pivotal in the development of the African-American spirituals. One spiritual conveying this message is:

> Steal away, Steal away,
> Steal away to Jesus!
> Steal away, steal away home,
> I ain't got long to stay here![10]

On the other hand, slaves created folktales as a strategy for coping with oppression, which became a profound sense of cultural cohesion among the men and women. They created an expressive system of coded messages to communicate what they considered good, worthy and meaningful.[11] Since slaves' survival depended on keeping their true feelings undetected in the presence of Whites, they employed the wit, intelligence, and ingenuity of Br'er Rabbit, Br'er Fox and others to resist and defeat the powerful foes: the master and his mistress.[12] This cultural form also served as a signifying form of resistance. One particular verse describes the proactive phenomenon of folktales in this way:

> Got one mind for white folks to see,
> Nother for what I know is me;
> He don't know, he don't know my mind.[13]

Katie Cannon (1995) crystalizes these ideas more succinctly, by stating:

> Living in a dialectical relationship with White Supremacy, folklore became an essential medium by which the themes of freedom, resistance, and self-determination were evoked, preserved, and passed by word of mouth from generation to generation. Older slaves used folktales to reveal to their fellow slaves what they knew. As tradition bearers, they instilled a way of knowing into instructional materials to teach younger slaves how to survive.[14]

As Cannon (1995) notes, these instructions and traditions as a system of resistance served to save lives and enabled slaves to move from bondage to freedom.

While there are few theories that discuss these acts of resistance, there are theoretical underpinnings that help to address African-American women's lives in their spirituality and resistance in the Academy today. The epitome of Black women's spirituality cannot ignore the ways an empowering form of resistance embodies their leadership approach. My conceptualization of the spiritual leadership of African-American women in the Academy has been influenced both by womanist theory, African-American literature on resistance, spiritual theories and qualitative studies on Black women leaders. I propose that the gestalt of Black women's existence and survival has been through their spirituality and resistance, which are woven together within the matrix of leadership. Such resistance can be explicated from various standpoints, including both spiritual and feminist theory by Cannon (1995), Collins (2000), Munro (1998), West (1988), and Stewart (1999).

Petra Munro (1998) acknowledges that there are two notions of the traditional concept of resistance, which have been defined in terms of opposition and power. Yet, Munro (1998) rearticulates ways in which resistance has been and can be a part of women's lives: " . . . resistance is not limited only to the use of non-hegemonic discourses, for hegemonic discourses can also be reconfigured and deployed to subvert each other."[15] In the same vein as Bettina Aptheker (1989), in *Tapestries of Life*, I posit that:

> Women's resistance comes out of women's subordinated status to men, institutionalized in society and lived through every day in countless personal ways. Women's resistance is not necessarily or intrinsically oppositional; it is not necessarily or intrinsically contesting for power. It does however, have a profound impact on the fabric of social life because of its steady, cumulative effects. It is central to the making of history . . . it is the bedrock of social change.[16]

Munro (1998) then adds: "Because women have traditionally been defined as objects, Nancy Miller (1989) maintains that women's relation to integrity and textuality, and to desire and authority, displays structurally important differences from the universal concept of resistance claimed by patriarchy."[17] Thus, it is from this standpoint that the very naming of ourselves is an act of resistance (Munro, 1998; Collins, 1991). Consequently, I posit that the subject of resistance for African-American women maintains a certain fluidity, which transcends their life histories and will be illuminated through their narratives. Notably, there are various cultural forms which exhibit ways African-American spirituality has served as a form of resistance and shaped our lives through music, dance, literature, oral histories, slave narratives, old 'Negro' spirituals, myths, folktales, and so on. For example, during slavery Africans were forbidden to congregate or communicate with each other; however, they used their spirituals as a form of resistance to communicate ways of survival or escape. Simultaneously, these spirituals served as a practice of freedom and hope to inspire one another to "hold on and stay strong" despite the oppressive forces they encountered on a day-to-day basis. Even today, African-American gospel music can be examined, and a strong sense of consciousness and feeling of spirituality can be evoked. The lyrics of "Hold on just a little while longer, everything will be alright," by the Sounds of Blackness (1994) demonstrates this notion.[18] A more recent song in today's pop culture is Mary Mary's (2000) "Shackles," which resounds with "Take the shackles off my feet so I can dance, I just wanna praise Ya . . . You broke the chains, now I'm gonna lift my hands, And I'm gonna praise ya, I'm gonna praise You."[19]

EMPOWERING RESISTANCE IN THE ACADEMY

Though I recognize there is an African-American ethos and ontology for how we know and see the world, what then does this mean for African-American women today in higher education? How are African-American women negotiating spaces and contesting the terrain walking the halls of the Ivory Tower? I would like to suggest several reasons that enable African-American women to sustain themselves in environments that contrast quite differently from their own cultural setting.

First, a deep sense of caring, moral authority, and freedom that struggles for justice creates a dramatically different political and intellectual ethos for African-American women. Hence, spirituality broadly defined continues to move countless African-American women to struggle onward in everyday life. In another sense, I would like to rearticulate the idea of "struggle" in everyday life to mean moving toward victory, toward higher ground, toward making inroads, toward achievement and success. Clearly, I must admit, many African-American women can be defined as struggling, yet I cannot say this is true for all African-American women. However, for those women who have chosen Academia as a career, the mere fact that we are here is contesting the terrain. We are creating our own path along the way, in a place traditionally not created for us, just as Sojourner Truth did over a century ago by creating her own identity and invoking naming as a symbolic act imbued with meaning. Born Isabella Baumfree, she dared to name herself after her emancipation. Refusing to be silenced, Truth claimed the authority of her own experiences to challenge various oppressive systems of her time such as racism, sexism, and class privilege.[20]

As noted by Sonia Sanchez in Collin's (1998) *Fighting Words*, "in addition to the necessity for us to be political, we must be spiritual . . . . Our spirituality will keep us from becoming cynical, from becoming bitter, from becoming harsh. Our politics combined with spirituality will keep us from becoming like the people that we are now trying to replace."[21] Unlike Sanchez, I am not advocating replacing anyone. However, like many other African-American women in the Academy, I am interested in creating spaces for groups of people who have been traditionally excluded from the decision-making process as well as creating spaces for those who have been traditionally marginalized.

In thinking about resistance, as I mentioned earlier, I am not using the traditional sense of resistance bearing upon the ideology of opposition and power, however, for the time being I have coined the term of "empowering resistance." Since African-American women's lives have been a part of a collective consciousness embodying our spiritual selves and our communities, the challenges and struggles thus have been redefined by empowering resistance. This type of resistance recognizes the obstacles, challenges and contestations of everyday life thus focusing more clearly on liberating the situation, moving through or over the obstacle (fluidity), and ultimately focusing on the victory. The spiritual self celebrates the victory and lives victoriously through our way of knowing and being.

An epistemological stance such as this focuses on moving forward by knowing what to do or finding ways to create those possibilities for change, wherein lies an ethos of the "nommo"—enacting the power of the spirit, activated through the spoken word. Nommo is acted upon through the use of one's spirit, thus symbolized in various forms, such as thought, music, drumming, song, dance, and so on. In articulating an empowering resistance, Marimba Ani (1980) would argue that nommo manifests itself in our ability to transform the English language to give it new life. We create and change our language according to our needs and circumstances of the Black ethos . . . . Our language expresses our ethos. It communicates our feelings and in doing [so], symbolically makes a statement about who we are. It defines our community.[22]

The History of Mary Prince, A West Indian Slave (1993), solidifies this notion of empowering resistance. Mary Prince, born a slave in Bermuda, took it upon herself to demonstrate outwardly acts of resistance. First, when Mary Prince ran away from her master after being beaten, her father returned her. But that particular day she stood up to her master by saying,

> I then took courage and said that I could stand the floggings no longer; that I was weary of my life, and therefore I had run away to my mother; but mothers could only weep and mourn over their children, they could not save them from cruel masters . . . . He told me to hold my tongue and go about my work, or he would find a way to settle me. He did not, however, flog me that day. [23]

Another form of empowering resistance occurred when Mary Prince got married without the permission of her slave owners. A third form of this resistance took place while Mary Prince was living with her master and his wife in England, when she was told upon several occasions to leave. After being told one time too many, she finally got fed up and left. In England, she was considered a free woman because of the abolition of slavery.

As I have discussed empowering resistance and its relationship throughout African-American women's history, we can take a journey by unfolding the pages of our past history and look at some of the women in higher education who have created a legacy and path for other African-American women today. Here, I offer a brief historical backdrop of the educational experiences of African-Americans in higher education, and then I present the lives and legacies of three women who have played a significant role in higher education during the late nineteenth and early twentieth centuries. The three women exemplars include: Lucy Diggs Slowe, Anna Julia Cooper, and Mary McLeod Bethune. Just as these women did almost a century ago, I conclude that the same holds true today in the way African-American women evoke the "nommo" and talk about their lives.

STONY THE ROAD WE TROD: A BRIEF HISTORY OF HIGHER EDUCATION FOR AFRICAN AMERICANS AND THE EXPERIENCES OF AFRICAN-AMERICAN WOMEN

In *The Education of Blacks in the South, 1860-1935,* historian James D. Anderson (1988) reveals that slaves and free blacks had already begun making plans for the systematic instruction of their illiterates "before northern benevolent societies entered the South in 1862, before President Abraham Lincoln issued the Emancipation Proclamation in 1863, and before Congress created the Bureau of Refugees, Freedmen, and Abandoned Lands in 1865. "[24] These early black schools were established and largely supported through African Americans' own resources. Some of these schools predated the Civil War and increased their activities after the war began. In September 1861, one of the first of these schools opened in Fortress Monroe, Virginia, under the leadership of Mary Peake, an African-American teacher. Another Black school had existed in Savannah, Georgia, under the leadership of "a black woman by the name of Deveaux," from 1833 to 1865, which was unbeknownst to the slave regime.[25] Deveaux quickly expanded her literacy campaign during and following the war.

During the early nineteenth century, the reasons for educating African-American women were the following: (1) to make good wives and mothers, and (2) to train good domestic servants and agricultural workers. In addition, African-American women were trained to become teachers, nurses, missionary workers, and Sunday school teachers in order to 'uplift the race'[26] Interestingly, as a part of the dialectical relationship Whites had with free Black men and women, Whites not only found it important to educate free Blacks, but Whites also imposed their own values by seeking to indoctrinate Black women on issues of morality, which would hopefully prevent them from falling prey to their 'natural inclinations.'[27] As such, the Bible was the pivotal point of instruction for African-American women. Again, the sole purpose of this kind of instruction was to impress upon the women the importance of living "'virtuous lives and to pass these values on to their children.'"[28]

In *Uplifting the Women and the Race*, Karen Johnson (2000) notes that Myrtilla Miner, a White woman from New York, founded one of the earliest educational institutions for Black women, in Washington, D.C. Though Miner received resistance from Whites, her school opened in 1851 and remained open, making it possible for a cadre of Black women to be trained as teachers. In turn, these teachers sought employment with the District of Columbia public schools and the surrounding area after emancipation.

By the latter half of the nineteenth century, Black colleges gained more prominence in training Black teachers. For instance, Fisk University in Tennessee, Hampton Institute in Virginia, and Tuskegee Institute in Alabama were established in the post-Civil War South, and most of these institutions enrolled women. Other schools built exclusively for Black women during this time were Scotia Academy, Spelman College, and Bennett College.

During these perilous times, African-American women teachers became the pillars of the Black community. Teaching provided one of the only viable professions possible. Johnson (2000) notes that Black women were excluded from male professions, along with the comparatively restricted areas opened to White women. Being a teacher in the African-American community gave rise to visibility that emerged as community leadership.[29] As noted by Darlene Clark Hine and Kathleen Thompson (1998), free African Americans continued to believe in the possibility of, as well as the necessity for, education. At the same time, teaching was not simply employment for Black women—it was an almost holy calling, an opportunity for service to the race.[30] Many times, Black professional women were able to get education and training only because a church or a community group paid their way; therefore, service to the community was African-American women's way of repaying the debt. Even when there was no tangible help available, Black women considered it a part of their job to serve the community; they believed it was their duty to themselves and their families to "advance the race."[31] Given that duty, teaching became an arena for political activism wherever it occurred.

We must not forget the role of the Black church, which was the heart of the Black community throughout the nineteenth and twentieth centuries, and which today still holds prominence in the African-American community. The church was often the only public building the community had access to, and in it took place not only religious services but classes, clubs, social events, and political meetings. For the most part, the leaders of the church were leaders of the community.[32]

The early beginnings of formal higher education for African Americans, particularly in the South, came on the heels of Reconstruction. Higher education was made available through private liberal arts colleges. As noted by Anderson (1988), "Between 1870 and 1890, nine federal land-grant colleges were established in the South, and this number increased to sixteen by 1915. In that same year, there were also seven state-controlled black colleges in the South."[33] Unfortunately, these normal schools or colleges were in name only, there was "only one of the sixteen black federal land-grant schools in the former slave states [that] taught students at the collegiate level."[34]

While African Americans, just having resettled their lives from an oppressive system of slavery, were attempting to make strides in education, White Americans were still trying to determine what would be best for them from an educational standpoint. Hence, the South was attempting to answer the question of whose interest would be served the best by these freed men, women and children? Dialectically speaking, the South had many contradictions to contend with as it related to "letting go," while wrestling with questions of what this education should be for the freed slave. In the midst of this were three separate and distinct philanthropic groups that formed the power structure of Black higher education during this period.[35] The first group were northern White benevolent societies and denominational bodies (missionary philanthropy). Second, there were Black religious organizations who established the beginnings of a system of higher education for Black southerners, and the third group consisted of large corporate philanthropic foundations and wealthy individuals. These groups had been involved in the development of Black common schools and industrial normal schools since Reconstruction, but in 1914 turned their attention to plans for the systematic development of a few select institutions of Black higher education.[36]

WE'LL LET NOBODY TURN US AROUND: THREE WOMEN EXEMPLARS FROM OUR PAST

While we are aware of some of the prominent African-American women educators of the nineteenth and twentieth centuries who were teachers, principals, and school founders, little is known about the role of African-American women educators in higher education. As aforementioned, education for African-American women is familiar ground since it was always one of the few respectable professions where they could gain access. In *Black Women in the Academy*, Nellie McKay (1997) notes "Still today, black women in education and all black people point with pride to a long list of distinguished black women educators from earlier times: Fanny Coppin, Lucy Moten, Frances Watkins Harper, Margaret Washington, Mary Church Terrell, and Anna Julia Cooper" are some of the best-known.[37] Without the efforts of many of these foremothers between the 1850's and the early part of this century, the African-American community would have never produced the women and men who held high the torch of freedom and literacy for Black people from the mid-nineteenth century through the 1950s and beyond.[38] Clearly, these foremothers provided the shoulders on which today's Black women educators stand. Still, there are many other African-American women of notable mention who made great contributions to the field of education. For the purpose of this project I will, therefore, focus on three particular women's lives that made significant contributions in the field of higher education during the late nineteenth and early twentieth centuries. Illuminating the lives of these women pioneers from our past aids us in understanding the depth of African-American women's presence in higher education, especially during a time when so few women were in leadership roles in this field. By briefly turning the pages back in history, I will share short biographical sketches on Lucy Diggs Slowe, Anna Julia Cooper, and Mary McLeod Bethune. These women's lives, leadership and spiritual presence lend it to understanding African-American women's leadership today.

Lucy Diggs Slowe

Born in Berryville, Virginia, on July 4, 1883, Lucy Diggs Slowe was orphaned by age five after the death of both parents. Slowe was raised by her paternal aunt, Martha Slowe Prince. In 1904, Slowe graduated as salutatorian in her class from the Baltimore Colored High School. She became the first woman graduate from her school to enter Howard University in Washington, D.C., and the first graduate to receive a college scholarship.

Slowe's interest in enhancing the quality and status of African-American women's lives in higher education was developed while she served as a student at Howard. "She was active in virtually every aspect of the university community and emerged as an outstanding leader on campus, participating in literary, musical, athletic, and social activities."[39] Though she has become well recognized for being one of the founding members of Alpha Kappa Alpha Sorority, the first Black Greek letter organization for women, her leadership accomplishments extend far beyond this significant endeavor. She also served as the first president of the sorority. In addition, she served as vice president and secretary of the Alpha Phi Literary Society, the first president of the women's tennis club, sang as a contralto with the university choir, and was a staunch supporter of the intercollegiate debate team.

Upon graduating from Howard in 1908 as class valedictorian, Slowe returned to her old high school in Baltimore to teach English. By 1916, Slowe had earned an MA from Columbia University, where she studied at Teachers College in the emerging field of Student Personnel.[40] The following four years (1916-20) proved to hold a successful teaching career for Slowe at Armstrong High School in the District of Columbia, where she taught English and also served as dean of girls. The quality of Slowe's work did not go unnoticed. In 1919, Slowe was requested by the District of Columbia's board of education to organize Shaw Junior High School, the first junior high for Blacks in the city where she was also appointed principal.[41] "In doing so, she called upon a faculty member from Teacher's College to teach an extension course on the junior high school for teachers of both races. This action was the first of many that demonstrated her high regard for the Teachers College faculty and also gave evidence of her efforts to foster integration."[42]

In 1922, Slowe was asked by Howard University's president J. Stanley Durkee to become the first dean of women, a position the female students had been requesting since 1913. Durkee was supportive of student activities and recognized its educational value, and he believed Slowe was someone who shared his philosophy. "Slowe did not accept Durkee's offer of employment immediately but negotiated for a higher salary and permission to live off-campus."[43] While she did not receive the salary request, she did receive permission to live off campus. As noted by Elizabeth L. Ihle (1994), this provision was important because it demonstrated already that Slowe had decided that a dean of women should be an educational leader rather than a student watchdog.[44]

Slowe's first few years at Howard witnessed a number of well-received innovations in women students' lives. One of her first actions as dean of women was extraordinary in the organizing of a Women Students' League. This league served as a student government association for every female student and all women automatically belonged upon registering at the university. Since few Black colleges at the time had any form of student government, establishing this activity for Black women was quite a radical move. Reasoning that women needed to get experience in working together for the common good, in decision-making, and in citizenship, Slowe thought that this league was an appropriate place to begin.[45] "Slowe's insistence that black college women understand American governance and be prepared to assist their communities reflected her larger concern for social justice."[46] Clearly, the purpose of organizing the Women's Student League was to develop student leadership.[47]

Following Slowe's appointment as dean of women, she also became president of the National Association of College Women (NACW). This organization was an outgrowth of the local D.C. College Alumnae Club, which consisted of classically trained and highly educated African-American women who were graduates of the leading White institutions in the nation and the two fully accredited Black colleges, Howard and Fisk Universities. Slowe continued to gain national prominence as she helped found the National Council of Negro Women and served as its first secretary. She founded the Conference of Deans and Advisors of Women of Colored Schools. In addition, she worked with the National Young Women's Christian Association and the Women's International League for Peace and Freedom. She also served on various boards of welfare agencies. Slowe's leadership in student personnel work gained such national prominence that she was well received by Black and White women on those college campuses that sought her advice and counsel on dealing with various issues concerning Black women students. In 1931, Slowe's stature as an outstanding leader in student personnel resulted in her being invited to speak at the predominantly White National Association of Women Deans. She was the first African-American to address this group.

As the first formally trained student personnel dean on a Black college campus, Slowe took the initiative to try to convince presidents of other Black institutions that this position was an important one and should be filled by a person formally trained with a BA degree, rather than the traditional "matron" who was usually appointed to police the morals of the women students. Slowe's assertiveness showed forth in many ways; it was one of her major goals to see the appointment of well-trained deans of women to appear on other Black college campuses.

Admittedly, Slowe was greatly influenced by the leading White women authorities on student personnel. Many of these scholars emphasized the idea that residential housing for women should not be mere places to reside, but centers for the development of the "total" woman, the "whole" student, and the women's leadership abilities. Slowe sought to bring this philosophy to Howard and to other black college campuses.[48]

During this tenure, Slowe was able to establish three new residence halls for women in 1931. In Slowe's desire to enhance women's cultural and leadership experiences it was important for her to stress the need for all women to live on campus, except those women who were residents of the District. "This was important for molding character and developing a sense of community, fellowship, leadership, and independence."[49]

Slowe found it just as important to impart the notion of leadership development to the female students since it was an expectation for the male students. She believed that self-government was vital to the development of good citizens and was critical of the administrators and faculty members who made most of the rules that students were expected to follow.[50]

According to Perkins (1996), one of the cornerstone's of Slowe's philosophy as dean of women was to impart to others that this was a professional position and not one of a caretaker or matron.[51] It was important for Slowe to exemplify this type of leadership as a model for women. Slowe became an outspoken advocate for treating Black women students with trust and respect, especially as it became apparent that the university was showing gender biases in the way they monitored the activities of women as opposed to how they monitored men. Slowe continuously voiced the need for African-American women to be in control of their lives and to develop leadership skills. Her leadership and desire to empower Black women students and faculty eventually put her at odds with Durkee's successor, Mordecai Johnson.

After Johnson became president, Slowe's leadership as dean of women began a downward spiral. During Durkee's administration, Slowe was a member of the President's Council of Deans, a position she lost in Johnson's administration. Her role of managing the residence halls was taken away and transferred to the University treasurer. To make matters worse, Johnson ordered Slowe to move from her home to Howard's campus to supervise the women on campus. In 1933, the entire women's program that Slowe had built during the first eleven years of her tenure was dismantled. Though these actions were touted as an economic measure, it gravely impeded important programs for female students such as the women's physician, dietician, director of dormitories, and the assistant to the Dean of Women. Slowe, however, protested these actions along with other alumnae and members of the National Association of College Women.

One of Slowe's ongoing battles with Johnson's administration occurred when she took a stand for the women students who alleged sexual harassment by one of the male professors at Howard. Unfortunately, matters only continued to get worse for Slowe; the administration took sides with Professor Mills, and Slowe's relationship with other male faculty deteriorated. Though Mills eventually left the university, "Slowe's difficulties with Johnson continued up to her death (which many of her friends believed to have been hastened by workplace stress)."[52]

Slowe's forthrightness in addressing moral and ethical issues of the time demonstrates a legacy of resistance. I would name it empowering resistance where she continued to stand firm in her beliefs, making considerable changes in the lives of women at Howard. In the broader national community, Slowe demonstrated leadership for other women to model in higher education. The name and life of Lucy Diggs Slowe can not go unnoticed in the history of higher education. Ihle (1994) sums up this idea of honor by stating that Slowe deserves scholarly recognition from professionals in student personnel work, feminists, and historians of education. "Her enlightened practices in student personnel work and her forward-looking attitudes about women and their place in both the university and society mark her as an activist and a thinker well ahead of her time."[53]

Anna Julia Cooper

Born a slave in Raleigh, North Carolina, the exact date of Cooper's birth is uncertain though several researchers have recorded dates from 1858 to 1860 (Guy-Sheftall, 1994; Johnson, 2000). According to Lemert and Bhan (1998), Cooper's date of birth is the most controversial date in her life history. However, Cooper's application for marriage (dated 11 June 1877) represents her age as nineteen, which would allow one to reasonably conclude that she was born in 1858.[54]

By 1868, Anna was awarded a scholarship to attend St. Augustine's Normal School and Collegiate Institute (previously the Normal School of North Carolina). St. Augustine's was founded in 1867 by the Board of Mission of the Episcopal church for the purpose of training teachers for newly freed slaves.[55] Early on, Anna questioned the way women were relegated to differential treatment by being excluded from taking Greek classes. Thus, she acquired a level of sensitivity towards such gender issues of the day and responded by boldly appealing to the principal and was granted permission to take the course. Anna completed her education in 1877, and remained at the school to tutor other students enrolled.

By age nineteen, Anna married Reverend George Cooper; he died two years later, and she remained a widow for the rest of her life. This unfortunate tragedy, however, did not deter her from continuing her education. Not only were Cooper's education and career important, but she also became a leader of social programs and causes for the poor in the District of Columbia. She was instrumental in establishing a local branch of the YWCA and was an early and lifelong leader in the social settlement movement.[56] In addition to Cooper's public life as a widow, she found time to rear seven children—two foster children when she was young, and five orphans she adopted just shy of her sixtieth year.[57]

In 1881, Anna enrolled in Oberlin College in Oberlin, Ohio, so that she could continue her teacher preparation and gain a more thorough education.[58] In 1884, she earned her A.B., and in 1887 the A.M. was awarded. Anna was quite fortunate to have attended Oberlin as during this time, few other colleges had opened their doors to women and Blacks.[59] Some of her extracurricular activities included memberships in the "LLS," a literary society for women, participation at "Thursday Lectures," and a series called "Generation X for women."[60] Also, Anna was involved in taking piano lessons; however, lack of funds and time inhibited her from pursuing her love of music as she would have liked.

When Anna graduated in 1884, she was among the first group of African-American women to earn a B.A. degree from Oberlin. In 1880,

Anna became the first principal of M Street High School for Colored Youth in Washington, D.C., a post she later reassumed in 1901. For a year, Anna taught at Wilberforce College in Xenia, Ohio, and then returned to her old school, St. Augustine's, to teach again. In 1887, Anna was awarded an M.A. in mathematics from Oberlin in recognition of her three years of teaching on the college level. Finally, Anna left St. Augustine's to teach at Washington Preparatory High School for Colored Youth (later M Street School and Dunbar High School).

Following the resignation of principal Robert Terrell from M Street High School, Cooper once again took over this leadership role and served from 1901-6. "During her tenure the school soared, the curriculum was strengthened, and accreditation was attained for the first time. She also initiated a college preparatory track and helped to obtain admission for M Street graduates to attend prestigious colleges such as Harvard, Brown, and Yale."[61]

Interestingly, a year-long controversy (1905-6) ended Cooper's career as principal in 1906. According to Lemert and Bhan (1998), White members of the District of Columbia's board of education joined together in the conspiracy to ruin Cooper's reputation and force her from the principal's office. The complaints were not of Cooper's curricular philosophy but supposedly of her failures as an administrator. When these attacks proved insufficient, Booker T. Washington's Tuskegee Machine resorted to fierce and scandalous tales about her. The Tuskegee operatives assuredly accused Cooper of a sexual liaison with one of her foster children. Unfortunately, these accusations magnified Cooper's life more intensely in the public eye. As noted in *The Voice of Anna Julia Cooper*, "It is not hard to imagine the mortification such preposterous charges must have caused a woman of Cooper's work ethic and impeccable morals."[62] Finally, Cooper was "dismissed in the fashion to which school administrators still resort . . . they simply did not renew her contract."[63] Despite these challenges, Cooper maintained her moral fortitude and went on to teach at Lincoln University in Missouri from 1906-11. When Cooper's rivals left the school administration office in Washington, D.C., she returned to the M Street High School in 1911, where she taught until her retirement in 1930.[64]

After retiring from the public schools, Cooper was named the second president of Frelinghuysen University, an evening school for Black working adults who could not have otherwise attended college. Cooper remained at Frelinghuysen for ten years.

At the age of sixty-five, Cooper earned her Ph.D. from the University of Paris, Sorbonne in 1925. This great accomplishment earned her the distinction of being the first African-American woman in Washington, D.C., to earn a Ph.D. at the Sorbonne, and she became the fourth African-American there to earn a doctorate.[65]

Guy-Sheftall (1994) sums up the 105 years of Dr. Anna Julia Cooper's life by stating:

> Never wavering from her philosophy of 'education for service,' she overcame every obstacle that the twin evils of racism and sexism put in her path. Her awesome intellect, high standards, unequivocal positions, and tenacity in the face of constant personal attacks both within the black community and beyond make her one of the most memorable figures in the annals of American education in the twentieth century. The educational reforms that she initiated at M Street (now Dunbar High School) and Frelinghuysen were pioneering. No less impressive was her persistent faith in the ability of African-American students to achieve excellence at their own institutions as well as at the most prestigious universities throughout the country. Perhaps Cooper's most significant legacy was her belief in the power of education to liberate and empower women to participate in the transformation of a world sorely in need of transformation.[66]

Mary McLeod Bethune

Born in 1875 near Mayesville, South Carolina, during the waning years of Reconstruction, Mary McLeod Bethune became a prominent figure in American history. Bethune was one of seventeen children born to the parents of former slaves. Bethune's earlier education began at a mission school, and afterwards she was awarded a scholarship to attend Scotia Seminary for Negro Girls in Concord, North Carolina. Six year of Scotia's highly regimented, Christian-centered learning environment led Mary McLeod Bethune to pursue a year of education at the Moody Bible Institute in Chicago, which is where she strengthened her inclination toward missionary work. However, after being rejected from a post in Africa, Bethune turned her zeal to education.

Several people in the educational arena were instrumental in Bethune's interest. One woman in particular was one of Bethune's former teachers, Miss Emma J. Wilson. Another person of great significance was the example set by Lucy Craft Laney, the founder of Haines Institute in Augusta, Georgia, where Bethune apprenticed from 1896-97. At the beginning of her teaching career, Bethune borrowed liberally from the teaching philosophies of her mentors Scotia, Wilson, and Laney. She applied Scotia's motto, "head, heart, and hand" to her mission of racial uplift. Furthermore, Scotia emphasized mental development, spiritual enrichment, and practical skills. Thus, graduates of her school were expected to conduct themselves in ways that reflected positively on the entire race, and they were encouraged to return to their communities to become exemplars of racial uplift and service to the masses of Black people.[67] In addition, Bethune shared Laney's philosophy that "educated black women should assume the 'burden' to uplift their families by providing moral, Christian leadership at home and in their communities, but she added to it a more politically tinged, female-centered activism."[68] Inherently, Bethune exemplified a lifelong commitment to improving the economic and political clout of Black women.

Mary McLeod married Albertus Bethune in 1898, and this union brought forth a son named Albert in 1899. Mary McLeod revealed very little about her nine years of married life. While she publicly agreed with Laney about the role of Black women in uplifting their families, her own life revealed a contradiction.[69] In 1907, Bethune's husband left the family, yet this did not stop her from pursuing her educational and activist life. For the sake of Bethune's reputation after the marriage dissolved, she never divorced, but instead declared herself a widow long before the death of Albertus in 1918.[70] Perhaps Bethune's strong sense of spirituality enabled her to endure the life of now being seen as a non-traditional woman while she pursued a very public life of education and politics.

In 1904, Bethune founded the Daytona Educational and Industrial School for Negro Girls, which carried out the mission of training African-American teachers for Florida's public schools. By 1923, Daytona Institute merged with Cookman Institute, a nearby men's school, and became the well-known Bethune-Cookman College.[71] Bethune served as president of this coeducational institution until 1942, and later served again from 1946-7. During this time, Bethune was also a highly visible leader in Black education and the Black women's club movement. Bethune served as president of the Florida Federation of Colored Women's Clubs (1917-25), where she founded a home for delinquent Black girls in Ocala, Florida. She also served as president of both the twelve-state Southeastern Federation of Colored Women's Clubs (1920-5) and the National Association of Teachers in Colored Schools (1923-4), a professional organization for Black teachers from mostly southern states.[72] Bethune gained greater national prominence when she defeated Ida B. Wells-Barnett for the presidency of the National Association of Colored Women. This position ensured Bethune, as national spokesperson, would be heard on major national issues concerning Black Americans. She served in this leadership role for two terms (1924-8). By 1935, Bethune founded the National Council of Negro Women, which was considered a more politically attuned organization.

Bethune's success in forging the way for Bethune-Cookman from its meager beginnings to collegiate status, plus her involvement in Republican politics, led to an invitation to attend a White House conference in 1930. Clearly, Bethune was a politician with both political parties, she was allied with the Republicans while they were in power; however, she became a partisan Democrat when she was tapped by Franklin Delano Roosevelt, along with Howard University president Mordecai Johnson, for the advisory board of the National Youth Administration. In 1936, Bethune became affiliated with the National Youth Advisory's Division of Negro Affairs, and as director she became the highest-paid African American in government.

"Bethune made her mark on the public discourse by utilizing lessons from her own family and schooling—self-help, pride and religious faith."[73] She was known for saying, "I have faith in God, and Mary Bethune."[74] Bethune was also known to be quite outspoken, and she held a firm belief that only a racially integrated America could safeguard Black rights, along with maintaining an intuitive sense of navigating the currents of the White power structure.

During the latter years of Mary McLeod Bethune's life, she created a foundation in her name, whose purpose was to house her papers and to promote her ideals of Black educational advancement, interracial cooperation, and service to young people.[75]

LOOKING TOWARD THE FUTURE

In spite of some of the unfortunate circumstances encountered by Lucy Diggs Slowe, Anna Julia Cooper, and Mary McLeod Bethune, it is clear their faith and perseverance kept them standing their ground in carrying out the leadership and service they felt "called to do." Clearly, their leadership in education and contributions to the African-American community overshadowed many of the adverse encounters they had to deal with in their careers. I would attribute much of their sense of spirituality to being able to withstand the various challenges they endured. Thus, this spirituality served as a form of empowering resistance, which allowed these women to move forward despite circumstances that may not always have served them favorable. Again, despite such challenges, these three women have left a chapter in history that must not go unnoticed. Admittedly, such adverse situations took a toll on the life of Lucy Diggs Slowe; however, she did not waver in her principles and stood her ground while patriarchal traditions reared their ugly heads. Ultimately, the high price paid for the service and leadership at Howard University came by never losing her dignity or self-respect while standing up to the patriarchal systems of domination. On the other hand, Anna Julia Cooper and Mary McLeod Bethune were able to withstand various challenges as it has been shown in their narratives. More importantly, I would like to suggest that these three women exemplars have paved a leadership path in higher education for the women in this study today.

Though the road has been "stony," African-American women have continued to withstand various forms of oppression on every level in the Academy, and the contemporary women in this study serve as a testament today contesting the terrain while walking the halls of the Ivory Tower. Despite such challenges, it has not caused them to waver in their life and leadership. Instead, much of the dialectical relationship between their spirituality and leadership has formed a transformational model of leadership that attributes to their success.

Once again, I am interested in focusing on the positive aspects of examining African-American women's lives in the Academy and how they make meaning of their spiritual selves in their everyday leadership practices on a day-to-day basis. How does their spirituality influence their work and the type of relationships they develop with others in the Academy?

At this point, I will shift forward to the contemporary women who have forged a similar path knowingly and unknowingly of their foremothers' leadership in higher education. The African-American women in this case study are deans of majority institutions. In a similar way, the lives of the three contemporary women in this study parallel the lives of the foremothers in that they have similar leadership traits, though, they were quite different in their character and style as it was exemplified in various settings socially, culturally and politically. The contemporary women's narratives are just as real as their foremothers, however, their names have been kept confidential for the sake of privacy on their part.

CHAPTER 2
Surveying the Literature

> The intellectual history of a people or nation constitutes to a great degree the very heart of its life. To find this history, we search the fountainhead of its language, its religion, and its politics expressed by tongue or pen, its folklore, and its songs.—Gertrude Bustill Mossell

EMBEDDED WITHIN THE FABRIC OF EVERY ORGANIZATION/INSTITUTION ARE power relations on every level vis-à-vis identity and cultural politics, which become a part of the lived culture of the web of people within these organizations. In many ways institutions help to define who we are and what we do. However, behind the veil of these institutions are the people who set the policies, develop ideologies and philosophies, rules and regulations, and so on. Thus, if organizations/institutions are serious about making change and creating space for those who have been traditionally marginalized, they must first address their own biases and stereotypes in order to better understand the many diverse cultures within their environment. This calls for a transformation in leadership. Hence, leaders must be willing to do the tough work, and make the deep changes within themselves, and become willing to lead by example.

As an African-American woman led by the "Spirit," I philosophically believe in developing relationships with people who show value and respect for various groups not based on race, class, gender, age, sexual orientation, and recognize people as human beings who are not monolithic, thus rejecting the traditional androcentric-patriarchal-individualistic leadership philosophy. In turn, leading by the "spirit" would create a web of relations, open to listening to the multiple voices within the organization, and creating spaces for greater collegiality to take place. Furthermore, as an African-American woman in the Academy, it is critically important to recognize the challenges that one would potentially face while standing at the helm.

First, however, it is necessary to identify my own position in the context of leadership as a Black Feminist/Womanist. Like Collins (2000), I ascribe to a holistic approach to leadership combining African humanism, feminism/womanism and spirituality as a way to transform our society, and more specifically the Academy. African humanism affirms that each individual is thought to be a unique expression of a common spirit, power, or energy inherent in all life.[1] Inherent in Black feminism is a process of self-conscious struggle that empowers women and men to actualize a humanist vision of community.[2] At the same time, we must continue to call attention to the "widespread acknowledgement that sexism, racism, and class exploitation constitute interlocking systems of domination,"[3] which must be the work of education for critical consciousness—to develop and make various strategies for participation and transformation a necessary agenda.[4] Thus, interwoven within this humanism and critical consciousness lies a spirituality that would help to transcend human ways of thinking and knowing. It would call for a moral consciousness to bring about harmony, justice and fairness for all people within the realms of the Academy. Thus, this spirituality calls for the "deep changes" (e.g. self-reflection, leading by example) by examining ways in which different groups can come together more or less in a "concentric circle," which espouses "power with versus power over" within the domains of the organization. Finally, "Black women intellectuals [including myself] who articulate an autonomous, self-defined standpoint are in a position to examine the usefulness of coalitions with other groups, both scholarly and activist, in order to develop new models for social change."[5]

In order to fully elucidate the phenomenon of African-American women's leadership and spirituality, I take a closer look at the lives of three African-American women deans. I integrate various theories to help make meaning of their leadership practices on a day-to-day basis. The theoretical frameworks that I draw upon include leadership theory (Benjamin, 1997; Bensimon and Neumann, 1993; Fairholm, 1997; Heifetz, 1994; Helgesen, 1990; Morgan, 1997; Wheatley, 1992), which helps me identify and make sense of various ways in which African-American women lead. Unquestionably, feminist and womanist theories (Collins, 2000; Guy-Sheftall, 1995; hooks, 1979; James and Busia, 1993), help to fully explicate Black women's ways of knowing and being, and how their lives have been shaped from a socio-cultural and socio-historical standpoint. At the same time, the trajectory of Black women's spirituality is further illuminated through spiritual theories (Ani, 1980; Ephirim-Donkor, 1997; Hopkins, 1999; Mbiti, 1991; Paris, 1995; Stewart, 1997 and 1999; Welch, 1999; West, 1999) and helps make meaning of African-American women's lived experience.

In *Black Women in the Academy: Promises and Perils*, Lois Benjamin (1997) offers provocative essays exploring the themes of identity, power, and change by thirty-three African-American women academics and administrators from around the country. These women's accounts collectively serve as an important work by providing a handbook for developing a framework for understanding the challenges and changes African-American women have endured while serving in the Academy. Helgesen's (1990) qualitative study on four women in various leadership roles offers a new paradigm for the way in which women lead and succeed in management. Admittedly, none of the women in Helgesen's study were leaders in higher education. In *Sister Power: How Phenomenal Black Women Are Rising to the Top*, Reid-Merritt (1996) offers in-depth interviews with more than forty-five Black female executives and how they are succeeding in edging their way through the glass ceiling. "We meet women who insisted on their right to self-identity, women who had to create themselves over and over again, women of vision who even now continue to challenge our sense of what is possible."[6]

LEADERSHIP THEORY

This study draws upon a variety of leadership theories that will help make sense of how African-American women lead in the Academy. In *Talking Leadership: Conversations with Powerful Women,* thirteen women concluded:

> . . . the world needed to change and that part of the job was up to them. Some of these women were conscious from the beginning that leading was what they were all about. Others came late, and with strong misgivings, to that awareness. In the end, however, all would agree that, at least, small groups of committed persons have played a critical role in changing the world and will doubtless continue to do so.[7]

One of these powerful women is Ruth J. Simmons, an African-American woman college president who discusses how she views her leadership and the influences of her success. Simmons comments on leadership, " . . . I think we should be teaching every individual in this society to take personal responsibility for contributing something, for bettering society in whatever way possible. I take this view largely because of what my mother taught me as a child."[8]

Fairholm's (1997), *Capturing the Heart of Leadership: Spirituality and Community in the New American Workplace*, serves as a critically important work for this study as it conceptualizes a new paradigm for leadership. Leaders today are asked to bring to the task of leadership their whole selves, which can not be done without recognizing the spiritual aspect of one's life, which is more powerful than any other force that guides their daily action.[9] Clearly, detailed knowledge of theory and practice in leadership is important, however, as Fairholm (1997) states, it is the spiritual knowledge that is essential. "It is what we are, who we are, and why we think we are here in life that ultimately guides our individual lives and conditions our relationships with others."[10]

In *The Drama of Leadership*, Robert J. Starratt (1993) metaphorically discusses leadership as drama, which occurs for both the individual leader, and the organization. According to Starratt (1993), "Leadership involves the playing of the drama with greater intensity, with greater risk, with greater intelligence and imagination, with greater dedication to making the drama work. One of the distinguishing qualities of a leader is the leader's passionate commitment to making the drama work better, and better for everyone involved."[11] Starratt (1993) posits that because the leader lives inside the drama more intentionally and with a more focused reflexive monitoring action, the leader is able to imagine greater possibilities for the drama, and to conjecture about ways to make that happen.[12] African-American women in leadership have been faced with the ongoing changes and challenges of the Academy to the extent of living the drama with intensity, taking risks, and looking at ways to positively affect human lives.

On the other hand, Morgan (1997) offers another view in looking at the way in which people lead. He offers various lenses describing what takes place within organizations. Several metaphors emerge which may be helpful in better understanding the ways in which African-American women make sense of their experience in the Academy. Such metaphors include the holographic design, culture, and political systems. The holographic design which may be least understood is based on five principles from building the whole of the organization into parts in helping the organization become a learning environment. Certain aspects of the holographic metaphor can be realized in practice by focusing on corporate culture, information systems, structure, and roles. Looking at the corporate culture/educational culture would be critical to any organization in order for it to maintain a healthy sense of purpose and stability. For example, the corporate culture embodies focusing on the visions, values, and sense of purpose that bind the organization together, which can be used as a way of helping every individual understand and absorb the mission and challenge of the whole enterprise.[13] In examining the culture lens, it is a process of reality construction that allows people to see and understand particular events, actions, objects, utterances, or situations in distinctive ways. "These patterns of understanding help us to cope with the situations being encountered and also provide a basis for making our own behavior sensible and meaningful."[14] In addition, " . . . recognizing that we accomplish or enact the reality of our everyday world, we have a powerful way of thinking about culture. It means that we must attempt to understand the culture as an ongoing, proactive process of reality construction. This brings the whole phenomenon of culture alive."[15] Along with this, political systems undergird every organization, and the greatest challenge has to do with how the politics are engaged and by whom. Morgan's political metaphor "encourages us to see organizations as loose networks of people with divergent interests who gather together for the sake of expediency" [e.g., making a living, developing a career, or pursuing a desired goal or objective].[16] I believe Morgan's metaphors are key in understanding African-American women's leadership and the trajectory of spirituality and how it is manifested in this leadership phenomenon.

Helgesen's (1995) study describes specific ways in which women lead. According to studies conducted by the Center for Values Research:

> . . . top women managers are more likely to be what the center characterizes as 'existential' leaders—that is, leaders who are able to reconcile a concern for bottom-line results with a concern for people; who focus on both ends and means; who are good at both planning and communication; and who are 'reality-based,' able to comprehend all the important aspects of existence—thus the term existential.[17]

Hegelsen's study focuses on four women in leadership describing the various ways in which they lead. By society and higher education learning more of the feminine principles, it gives women unique opportunities to assist in the continuing transformation of the workplace—"by expressing, not by giving up, their personal values."[18]

When specifically discussing women in higher education and leadership, Bensimon and Neumann (1993) note that recent scholarship on the moral development of women merits consideration as a theoretical base for the reconceptualization of leadership as a collective and interactive act. Here, they offer:

> This is because it is grounded in the experience of people—women—whose backgrounds differ dramatically from the norm of leadership, which is male dominated and heavily individualistic in orientation. We believe that this body of knowledge about women, about women's ways of knowing and thinking, and about efforts to liberate that thinking, is particularly relevant to a reconceptualization of leadership based on the theme of inclusive teamwork . . . . [19]

More specifically, I posit that learning more about the ways in which

African-American women use their spiritual leadership may provide a unique lens which higher education can adopt in order to help transform the Academy.

As previously noted, I use various leadership theories to serve as a framework for how we look at the characteristics of African-American women's leadership styles. Metaphors such as Starratt's drama and Morgan's holographic design, culture, and political systems will assist in helping us to understand the leadership of African-American women. The conceptualization of Fairholm, Helgesen, and Bensimon and Neumann's framework for leadership will help to broaden the scope of understanding the ways African-American women lead.

FEMINIST/WOMANIST THEORY

Many African-American women have found it necessary to identify themselves beyond the general labels: feminist to Black Feminist, Womanist, Africana Womanist, and so on. Collins (2000) offers several reasons for Black women's self-definition in *Black Feminist Thought* which says, "First, our experiences as African-American women provide us with a unique standpoint on Black womanhood unavailable to other groups . . . it is more likely for Black women as members of an oppressed group to have critical insights into the conditions of our own oppression than it is for those who live outside those structures."[20] Second, Collins (2000) states that Black women intellectuals provide unique leadership for Black women's empowerment and resistance.[21] Forthrightly, these identity politics have been necessary since African-American women must address the interlocking systems of domination—race, class, and gender oppression. Thus, Collins (2000) states that Black feminist thought cannot challenge race, gender, and class oppression without empowering African-American women.[22] As noted by Quantz (1992) "culture is analyzed . . . not simply as a way of life, but also as a form of production that always involves asymmetrical relations of power, and through which different groups in their dominant and subordinate positions struggle to both define and realize their aspirations."[23]

Traditional mainstream feminism has ascribed to addressing gender oppression first and foremost and argued to some degree that this should be the only concern or the concern of priority. Unfortunately, African-American women cannot afford to solely address issues based on gender bearing in mind the social, political and historical construct of racism in America, and the underpinning remnants of slavery for people of African descent. In addition, Western feminism traditionally has been known to separate itself from men, which has resulted in a backlash to some degree. However, African-American women can not afford to separate themselves from men, since their cultural way of being is communal, which includes women, men, children, elders and extended families. Quite clearly, Quantz (1992) makes it plain by stating, "culture is not so much the area of social life where people share understandings as that area of social life where people struggle over understanding."[24] Thus, African-American women in the Academy keep the interest of the family and community alive through their research, scholarship, and dialogue. This departs from the Academy's elitist notion of how it defines scholarship.

hooks (1989) radically addresses the need to rethink the discussions of feminism in a form including those who may not engage on the academic level, which would be the grassroots politics of feminism. hooks offers:

> The separation of grassroots ways of sharing feminism across kitchen tables from the spheres where much of the thinking is generated, in the academy, undermines the feminist movement. It would further the feminist movement if new feminist thinking could be once again shared in small group contexts, integrating critical analysis with discussion of personal experience. It would be useful to promote anew the small group setting as an arena for education for critical consciousness, so that women and men might come together in neighborhoods and communities to discuss feminist concerns.[25]

This grassroots politic deeply departs from traditional feminist discourse in the Academy and other elite organizations. In turn, hooks' grassroots politics is holistic by addressing the concerns within the community and creating spaces for marginalized groups to become connected through holding various discussions. Culture, therefore, is a contested terrain with multiple voices expressed through constitutive power relations.[26]

Moreover, African-American women also recognize the need to address their "whole" selves as they relate to the triple oppression of race, class, and gender. Bearing this in mind, one issue is not necessarily given more "weight" over the other since it may not be clear what form of oppression is in operation at any given time. hooks (1989) addresses this by stating:

> Small groups of people coming together to engage in feminist discussion, in dialectical struggle make a space where the "personal is political" as a starting point for education for critical consciousness can be extended to include politicization of the self that focuses on creating understanding of the ways sex, race, and class together determine our individual lot and our collective experience.[27]

Once again, it's not only important for African-American women to address their whole selves (e.g. race, class, gender) in this patriarchal society, but it's just as important for them to address issues that impact every aspect of their lives, which includes their communities—families, extended families and men. Moreover, Collins (2000) distinctly answers the question of "What is Black feminism?" by summing up the ideas of Anna Julia Cooper, Pauli Murray, bell hooks, Alice Walker, Fannie Lou Hamer, and other Black women intellectuals. "Inherent in their words and deeds is a definition of Black feminism as a process of self-consciousness struggle that empowers women and men to actualize a humanist vision of community."[28] Henceforth, a humanist vision involves fundamental democratic and moral imperatives.

Although African-American women's identity politics distinguishes themselves from mainstream feminism, they recognize that while Black feminist thought may originate with Black feminist intellectuals, it cannot flourish isolated from the experiences and ideas of other groups.[29] "The dilemma is that Black women intellectuals must place our own experiences and consciousness at the center of any serious efforts to develop Black feminist thought yet not have thought become separatist and exclusionary."[30] Yet, it is clear that coalitions also require dialogue with other groups. Furthermore, Collins (2000) points out that this humanist vision is also reflected in the growing prominence of international issues and global concerns in the works of contemporary African-American women intellectuals.[31]

Collins (2000) ascribes to a holistic approach to leadership combining African humanism, feminism/womanism and spirituality as a way to transform our society, and more specifically the Academy. African humanism affirms that each individual is thought to be a unique expression of a common spirit, power, or energy inherent in all life.[32] Inherent in Black feminism is a process of self-conscious struggle that empowers women and men to actualize a humanist vision of community.[33] Simultaneously, we must continue to call attention to the "widespread acknowledgement that sexism, racism, and class exploitation constitute interlocking systems of domination,"[34] which must be the work of education for critical consciousness—to develop and make various strategies for participation and transformation a necessary agenda.[35] Thus, interwoven within this humanism and critical consciousness lies a spirituality that would help to transcend current human ways of thinking and knowing. It would call for a moral consciousness to bring about harmony, justice and fairness for all people within the realms of the Academy. This spirituality calls for "deep changes" (e.g. self-reflection, leading by example), it calls for examining ways in which different groups can come together more or less in a "concentric circle," which espouses "power with versus power over" within the domains of the organization. Finally, "Black women intellectuals (including myself) who articulate an autonomous, self-defined standpoint are in a position to examine the usefulness of coalitions with other groups, both scholarly and activist, in order to develop new models for social change."[36] Inherent in this exercise is learning the ways that social change can become attainable through listening to the voices of African-American women and how they have been helping to change the Academy in their own spaces.

SPIRITUAL THEORIES

Ironically, an emerging body of literature on spirituality in organizations and the workplace has surfaced within mainstream discourse (Palmer, 1999; Welch, 1999; Wheatley, 1994); yet spirituality has been central in the lives of African-American women throughout history in this country. On the other hand, there is another body of literature continuing to emerge on and about African-American spirituality (Ani, 1997; Dash, Jackson, & Rasor, 1997; Hull, 2001; Stewart, 1999), which helps to inform our cultural and spiritual way of knowing and being. Similar to other groups such as Native Americans and Asians, African-Americans have maintained a strong sense of spirituality. This spirituality played a formidable role in sustaining the lifeblood of African peoples who were enslaved in America. Religious notions and practices, however, came about at a later point, since slaves were not allowed to congregate for church gatherings and worship. Thus spirituality sustained Africans' belief of the existence of a Supreme Being who was "Just" despite their enslavement. Such a belief became a form of liberation to Africans, which in turn enabled them to sustain themselves against the hostility and wickedness of slavery.

It is critically important to explicate the distinction between the spirituality of African peoples versus an Eurocentric spirituality. The African view of God is covenantal . . . God is viewed as reciprocally related to the tribal community.[37] This distinction has been elucidated by Peter J. Paris (1995):

> . . .[O]nce the African slaves had discovered that the biblical God had taken initiative in forming covenantal relationship with a band of slaves in Egypt and had promised to lead them to freedom in return for their obedience and faithfulness, they knew that that God was not the possession of slaveholders but, rather, the latter's opponents. That discovery made possible easy acceptance of the Christian worldview because it meshed so well with their traditional African understandings of a tribal deity. Further, African-American Christianity enabled the slaves to deepen their experience of racial unity of giving them the basic elements for the constitution of a new myth of origin wherein the major biblical personages were transformed and began functioning much as African ancestors had inspired them to greater devotion. Further still, their clandestine ritualistic gatherings and liturgical practices of worship became the locus for syncretising African and

> Christian worldviews into a dynamic unified whole. Thus, in the midst of their suffering, Africans discovered that they had not left God on the continent with their material cultural artifacts, but had discovered their God anew in this alien land inhabited by such a cruel people. In continuity with their African experience, this God constituted the ultimate grounding for their understanding of human nature and the organizing principle for their associational life. Their Christian belief that God wills that the good of all peoples should be realized in community (that is, in harmony with others) is both commensurate with and expansive of the African traditional understanding of God.[38]

As described by Paris (1995), African [and African-American] ways of knowing and recognition of God as a Supreme Being is evidenced through their spirituality. Furthermore, this spirituality was embedded in a deep-rooted connection with community. Such "cosmological connectedness" departs from Eurocentric spirituality, which has traditionally been embedded in materialistic and individualistic ways of knowing.

While there are key differences between African spirituality and Eurocentric spirituality, there is a tangential connection between Wheatley's (1994) new science, African spirituality and the "new" leadership theories on spirituality. The holism that exists in all three ontological discourses is fundamental to the core of this spirituality. Organizations have been challenged to do more than recognize their people as mere workers or mechanized entities, but as humans with a human connection—mind, body, and soul.

As noted by Palmer (1999), "Spirit is. Consciousness is. Human awareness is. Thought is. Spirituality is. Those are the deep sources of freedom and power with which people have been able to move boulders and create change."[39] Palmer continues by describing a leader as "a person who must take special responsibility for what's going on inside him or her self, inside his or her consciousness, lest the act of leadership create more harm than good."[40]

In *Deep Change*, Quinn (1996) refers to such leadership by saying, "To bring about deep change, people have to suffer the risks. And to bring about deep change in others, people have to reinvent themselves."[41] Thus, in order for people to lead organizations, they must ultimately know within themselves what they're made of. Quinn (1990) describes this important link between deep change at the personal level and deep change at the organizational level by stating:

> To make deep personal change is to develop a new paradigm, a new self, and one that is more effectively aligned with today's realities. This can only occur if we are willing to journey into unknown territory and confront the wicked problems we encounter. This journey does not fol-

> low the assumptions of rational planning. The objective may not be clear, and the path to it is not paved with familiar procedures. This tortuous journey requires that we leave our comfort zone and step out side our normal roles. In doing so, we learn the paradoxical lesson that we can change the world only by changing ourselves. This is not just a cute abstraction; it is an elusive key to effective performance in all aspects of life.[42]

Hagberg (1994) has elucidated 'leading from within' in another way, articulating leadership as having the ability to lead from the soul. "The endpoint of leadership is not just the position of power we reach, but the continual change and deepening we experience that makes a difference in our lives, our work, our world. Our leadership journeys are only at midpoint when we have achieved a position of power."[43] Hagberg (1994) continues by stating:

> The leadership journey is a matter of the soul and that is where the energy and the focus have to be . . . I am describing a different type of leadership than we are accustomed to. Leading from your soul involves things like meaning, passion, calling, courage, wholeness, vulnerability, spirituality, and community. It does not represent the traditional forms of leadership and it goes beyond the new feminist forms, intriguing as they are. This leadership, which I call soul leadership, transcends both masculine and feminine forms, reaching to another level, in which we connect our souls, our cores, and our essence.[44]

Leadership from "within" and from the "soul," quite clearly, is a new form of leadership that was unthinkable in organizations ten years ago. Hagberg (1994), therefore, raises the question as to why is it necessary to have leaders who lead from their souls, people who can operate from a place of inner peace? She answers this question by saying, "Because the future requires leaders who do not operate out of fear or ego gratification, who do not revert to traditional authoritarian styles when things get tough, who do not have to prove their worth by supplying the answers."[45] Hagberg (1994) goes a step further by quoting Rob Harvey in the introduction of her book:

> Leadership always comes back to the issue of character, of deep foundational values. In the current reformation this country is experiencing, and the instability we are feeling, you cannot lead by forcing compliance. It simply doesn't work. The rate of change is too high to be managed from the top down. In order to lead, one must engage followers. You will not find followers without caring, connecting, and creating. Would you follow someone who did not care about you, connect with you, or did not wish to create a new reality? Mere compliance today is

> a recipe for disaster. As leaders, or would-be leaders, we must be vulnerable. None of us has arrived. We must recognize our own voyage. We can only lead effectively by enabling others to maximize their contribution. We are all on the journey together, accomplishing things that none of us could accomplish alone.[46]

Similarly, leadership can be defined as the shared construction of meaning. "Leadership requires the skill in the creation of meaning that is authentic to oneself and to one's community. It also requires the uncovering of meaning that is already embedded in others' minds, helping to see what they already know, believe and value, and encouraging them to make new meaning."[47] Likewise, Rogers (1999) notes Drath and Palus view of leadership as meaning-making in a community of practice. Leaders are "the people who are able, for reasons of intelligence, knowledge, experience, to express formulations of meaning on behalf of a community—they can say what people have in their minds and hearts."[48]

Once again, the "connection to spirituality here is that leaders can create a framework of understanding in a community that promotes the values of justice, peace and the common good, or they can instill a spirit of despair."[49] The point, however, is that the ground on which the leader stands co-creating environments or making meaning of a community's experience is a tremendously significant part of the leadership equation. "To the extent that the leaders struggle to understand and accept their inner limitations and understand how their fears can impact the conditions they create and the meaning they make, dictates whether they cast 'shadow or light' on the world around them."[50] The key question here is . . . What are some ways in which people can develop their inner spirit in order to move to the consciousness of "soul" leadership?

Hagberg (1994) suggests ways in which people can develop soul leadership. First, she states that in order to transform organizations we need to transform ourselves. We have to become whole, which is "a profoundly spiritual journey requiring courage."[51] "It requires a leap of faith to lead from our souls. It requires courage: a conscious reflective decision to act on life-giving principles, despite the consequences, even if they threaten our priorities or existence . . . Courage is what we develop on this journey to soul leadership. It takes us into new territory. It allows us to go beyond what we were capable of saying and doing before. We go to our depths and find our heights, and in our lives we emerge as wise leaders."[52]

As with the new science and womanist leadership, we must be connected with the whole, connected with the complex inner makings of self to help further the connections with the external—the people around us, within our organizations and our communities. Ultimately, soul leadership is communal; it is a process in which we grow more with the divine to have the capacity to grow within the communities around us. Clearly, it is impossible to predict how each person will experience the journey to soul leadership; which is why the journey is a process. "The process is as important as the destination. In fact, the process may be the destination."[53] There are a few characteristics that emerge universally in people who have taken the inner journey described. "They have peace even in chaos, they are clear and undiluted, they are compassionate, they are courageous, and they listen to their calling . . . Soul leaders will change the world."[54]

While an emerging body of literature on spirituality in organizations has developed over the past ten years, there has not been a concurrent body of literature to emerge on African-American women's spirituality in organizations and the ways in which they have influenced the inner workings of organizations. I posit that many of these same African-American women have had an influence on some of these scholars who now write about spirituality and have become more comfortable with the subject in public circles. The growing body of literature on Black women's feminist discourse serves as a framework and a catalyst to produce the body of literature on Black women's spirituality within organizations. Admittedly, Black women's spirituality is mentioned in various ways in feminist/womanist discourse, yet it is still not elucidated to the extent of understanding the ways in which this spirituality manifests itself for African-American women in leadership within organizations, particularly in the Academy. As I have identified scholars producing work on spirituality in the Academy and the lack of writings on African-American women, it has inspired me to give "voice" to these women who have played a critical role in feminist/womanist discourse, education and society, and the Academy.

In this study, I hope to bring forth a body of literature that will help us to better understand the spiritual leadership of African-American women, and how their leadership may serve as a model for transforming the Academy.

CHAPTER 3
Methodology

> As subjects, people have the right to define their own reality, establish their own identities, [and] name their history—bell hooks

AS MENTIONED IN CHAPTER ONE, THIS CASE STUDY EXAMINED THE LIVES of three African-American women in higher education administration. More specifically, the purpose of this study is to examine the ways in which African-American women make meaning of their spiritual selves in their everyday leadership practices. In this qualitative case study, strong cultural and phenomenological interests dominate in the meaning-making process of these women's lives. Robert Stake (1994) offers that a case study emphasizes drawing attention to the question of what can be learned from a single case.[1] In this particular study, there is much to be learned in the "boundedness" of examining the spiritual leadership of the three women. By examining their spiritual leadership, it helps the reader to better understand the ethos of these African-American women and how spirituality has influenced their work and the type of relationships they have developed with others in the Academy. Another consideration is to elucidate the way these women have negotiated spaces of difference through their spiritual leadership and how they impact the social, cultural, and political construct of a male-dominated arena.

While I have continued to examine the various theoretical frameworks on leadership, feminism/womanism and spirituality, it should come as no surprise that feminist methodology would inform the discursive practices in the way this study has been conducted. Examining the various theories—leadership, feminist/womanist and spiritual—drives this research to raise critical questions and move toward a liberatory praxis for educators and administrators in higher education. Since I am interested in understanding the intersubjectivities of African-American women's spiritual leadership and how they make meaning of their lives in the Academy, I believe a qualitative study serves as the best way to gain the multiple perspectives of these women. I draw heavily upon the work of feminist/womanist sociologist and scholar Patricia Hill Collins, whose work not only addresses the positionality of African-American women culturally, socially and politically, but also addresses the ways spirituality has impacted their lives historically. Collins (2000) notes the imperatives of doing research about Black women by having them assert their own standpoint and speak for themselves as an oppressed group. Collins (2000) offers, "First, our experiences as African-American women provide us with a unique angle of vision concerning Black womanhood unavailable to other groups, should we choose to embrace it."[2] Furthermore, Collins (2000) asserts, "It is more likely for Black women, as members of an oppressed group, to have critical insights into the condition of our oppression than it is for those who live outside those structures."[3] Feminist scholar bell hooks (1989) offers "As subjects, people have the right to define their own reality, establish their own identities, [and] name their history."[4] From a qualitative research perspective, it is critically important that African-American women are centered as the subjects of their own research. In support of this notion, Teresa Fry Brown (2000) notes that the literature of African-American women mirrors their life experience. Brown (2000) continues by stating,

> Articulation of the realities of black womanhood and sharing what they have learned about how to conduct themselves are essential to the subsistence of the black woman, black family, black church, and black community. Autobiographical and biographical writings are distinct indicators of how African-American women transmit values intergenerationally.[5]

In a similar vein, Petra Munro (1998) advances research on writing about women's lives when she talks about teachers by saying that to conduct the life histories of women teachers is to take seriously the lives of women teachers. By taking their stories seriously, one must acknowledge their conversation as more than just 'idle talk' or mere gossip. Alice Walker frames women's stories as 'mystories'; which exemplify stories of the way women know themselves.[6] Munro (1998) notes that Carol Christ reminds us that the simple act of telling a woman's story from a woman's standpoint is a revolutionary act. By "naming the gap between men's stories about women and women's own perception of self and world" women's narratives become a generative space for understanding not only the complexity of women's lives but how women construct a gendered self through narrative.[7] In turn, this means including aspects of women's life stories that have traditionally been dismissed, which is what we as women can no longer afford to do.

In further advancing the discourse of how we talk about women's lives, Munro (1998) offers the following:

> The manner of the telling, the authoring of oneself through story, provides a space for understanding what Bakhtin (1981) calls the dialogic of self, the relationship between self and culture. In situating women teachers as 'authors' (Casey), their narratives can suggest the meanings they give to their lives. How individuals construct their stories, the tensions, the contradictions and the fictions, signifies the very power relations and discursive practices against which we write our lives. Thus, the use of language—the myths, metaphors and imagination—in the way that individuals construct a self is a political act [Personal Narrative Group 1989; Portelli, 1993].[8]

In the same vein, Linda Thompson (1992) recognizes the ways in which several feminist epistemologies work together to inform women's research. Three particular tenets discussed by Thompson include: (1) value-sustaining and political inquiry; (2) connection between researcher and researched; and (3) women's experience as source and justification of knowledge. First, feminists believe that science is a social activity embedded in a socio-historical context and shaped by personal concerns and commitments. The neglect and distortion of women's lives, coupled with the sexist bias in social science research, make it critical to place women's stories at the center. "All research sustains beliefs and politics whether or not they are acknowledged."[9] Therefore, a feminist standpoint would reject any notion of objectivity founded on the possibility of knowledge being untainted by history, culture, politics, and personal beliefs. Hence, research for women is emancipatory; feminism is an ideology and a political movement for social change.

Second, there is a connection between the researcher and the researched. Constructed knowers weave together what they know from their own personal experience with what they learn from others; thus moving beyond academic disciplines and their methods as the sole source of authority, and reclaiming themselves as sources of knowledge.[10] Constructed knowledge requires reflexivity (Thompson, 1992); this in turn requires the knower to reflect on her/his own thoughts, moods, desires, and judgments while continuously posing questions to her/himself and pushing at the boundaries of his/her self-awareness.[11]

Third, Thompson (1992) notes that to speak from experience has authority. For many feminists, it is quite unsettling to remove their own experience from the research process (Thompson, 1992). "Many feminists celebrate experientially-based knowledge by making the everyday experience and language of women—including themselves—the source and justification of "truth" (Thompson, 1992). Hence, women become the creators and the substance of knowledge.

Consequently, this project has not been an exercise of merely collecting data and recording what participants have to say through a process of disinterestedness. My own experience working in higher education, both within the Ebony and Ivory Towers, offers a perspective/lens which allows me to question how other women have navigated their way through their leadership path while recognizing the unrelenting oppressive forces that can be operating on any given day. Yet, we cannot afford to hide the realities of these forces; thus we must address ways we can create a liberatory practice of freedom for those to come. As I have previously stated, African-American women's lives cannot be talked about without recognizing the ways in which spirituality has had an impact on their lives and their leadership. Again, I reiterate that as we talk about spirituality in medicine, business, education, and other arenas, it must also be revealed through the eyes of African-American women in leadership. The Academy is a good place to begin this dialogue.

Benjamin's (1997) collection of essays in *Black Women in the Academy: Promises and Perils,* offers multiple voices of the lives of African-American women in the academy, who share their stories of what walking the halls of the Ebony and Ivory Tower have been like for them. This important study helps to lay a framework for understanding the changes and challenges African-American women have endured while serving in Academia. Not only does this multivoclivity show us some of the challenges of African-American women's experiences, but it is also inspirational by providing success stories of those women who have contested the terrain and succeeded against the odds. Yet, these stories have not unfolded without addressing the ways in which the triple oppression of race, class, and gender have been embedded within the matrix of everyday life for African-American women. Though some women may have experienced more tensions with race, versus gender or class, others may have experienced all three factors on any given day. What in turn does one do when recognizing various tensions that may be operating without losing a sense of self?

Notable scholars Patricia Hill Collins (2000), bell hooks (1989), and Stanlie James and Abena Busia (1993) address African-American women's feminisms and their way of knowing and being which allow us to better understand how Black women strategically negotiate their space and maintain their place in the academic world. At the same time, the narratives of the three women in this study will offer how they have acquired and maintained their success by interweaving their spirituality into their leadership practices, thus offering a more pragmatic model of leadership. Like the foremothers mentioned earlier in this study, these women's lives by no means become monolithic, though, they all possess the commonality of spirituality as the core of their leadership.

I would like to reiterate that it is not my interest as a researcher to remain "disinterested" in how the three African-American women share their stories and talk about the spiritual nature of their lives and how they make-meaning and construct their own leadership paradigm, which ruptures the traditional mode of leadership practices. By disrupting the traditions of a hierarchical and mechanistic leadership paradigm, it is evident that these African-American women's leadership and spirituality play out in a dialectical nature, both phenomena informing one another. In essence, African-American women are unable to separate their spirituality from the way they lead and the relationships that they develop and encounter on a day-to-day basis.

Bearing this in mind, it is important as a researcher to address my own interests and "situated character," which has been done explicitly in this research. As the research unfolded, it was then determined where I would integrate my voice. This self-reflexivity must acknowledge that the knowledge being produced is inevitably limited by my own history, and the institutional forms within which I work. The capacity of self-reflection, therefore, could enable me to gain insights of social and cultural practices that may not have been a part of my initial awareness.

Thus, at the forefront of a critical project, one asks, whose interests are being served? Not only whose interests, but *how* are those interests being served? What are the ways in which African-American women make sense of their spirituality, and how is that interwoven into their leadership? How are their moral and ethical values congruent with what they say about the world of higher education and what they are required to do? Ultimately, how are these women using their approach to leadership to transform the Academy to the extent of making change based on sound principles without sacrificing themselves for the status quo?

Once again, as noted in *Ethnography and Qualitative Design in Educational Research*, "Researchers seek personal narratives and life histories to illuminate how people, particularly those from oppressed groups, construct their identities over time."[12] Thus, ethnography should not be based on the researcher's "understanding" (which places him or her in a privileged interpretive position) but in a "dialogue" between the researcher and the natives, in which both participants in the dialogue are an integral part of the study.[13] Clearly, my interest in this dialogue becomes more evident throughout various points of this research process.

In the undertaking of qualitative research it is important to note, "at the root of in-depth interviewing is an interest in understanding the experience of other people and the meaning they make of that experience."[14] Similarly, the discursive practices of interpretive discourse often place understanding (*Verstehen*) at the center of the conversation. "Understanding" refers to the way a particular group makes sense of their world rather than a set of laws fit to scientific theory.[15] While at the same time I acknowledge Quantz's (1992) position as he discusses critical research which "should serve the interest of emancipation, the researcher should not seek out or report only empirical evidence that supports the researcher's view. All cultural evidence needs to be observed, described, analyzed, and that which appears to counter researcher assumptions must be revealed."[16] Clearly, this research is not a mere exercise of collecting data and reporting what the participants have to say; I not only turned the mirror on myself, but also questioned and clarified various assumptions made throughout this research process.

DATA AND ANALYSIS

Since the topic of spirituality is still emerging in locations of the Academy and would have been virtually unheard of ten to fifteen years ago, it is critically important to clearly articulate the ways in which I am examining African-American women's leadership and how they make meaning of their lives.

I got started on this journey of exploring African-American women's leadership when I listened to African and African-American women talk about their spiritual selves and being connected with a church institution. I chose to explore this topic further as I reflected upon my own life and experience working in higher education and other organizations and thinking about my own way of knowing and being in the world. One critical signifier when talking with other women of African descent was the language they used to describe their spiritual selves, often referring to or recognizing a higher power for the reason they do the work they have chosen to do, which is what Khaula Murthada referred to as "God-talk." Then, after examining the literature in my *Transformative Leadership* course, these ideas began to merge in thinking about the ways African-American women talk about their lives and leadership. Consequently, as I explored the literature discussing African-American women's leadership, the notion of spirituality embedded in their leadership was alluded to, but not fully explicated in a way where African-American women talked about how they make meaning of their lives and leadership in this way.

In turn, this led me to conduct a pilot study using a focus group method of three African-American women leaders in Higher Education. Though this method proved beneficial, as it validated some of my initial assumptions, I found it to be somewhat stifling because it did not allow the women to fully reflect upon their experiences. Therefore, I decided to use Siedman's (1998) three-part interviewing process as a way to conduct this study.

SELECTION OF PARTICIPANTS

The women selected for this study were determined through referrals from various leaders in higher education. First, I asked various administrators and faculty members in higher education for recommendations of women who might possibly "fit" this study. After compiling a list of names, I developed a preliminary letter and questionnaire for the potential participants. Admittedly, I initially had in mind "high-profile" names for this study, such as well-known African-American women who either were or had served as college presidents. On the other hand, as I know and have known for most of my life, it is not the name that is most important; it is the authenticity of the individual that makes the biggest difference.

Having found the women who became a part of this study proved to be serendipitous by the way their stories unfolded, fully explicating how their spirituality and leadership were inextricably woven together. Therefore, I am truly blessed having found the women who agreed to offer their time, talent, and energy in making this research study a success. Assuredly, it is not the name or the title of the person that counts the most; it has more to do with the contributions of these three women's stories, their authenticity and how they have kept it "real" while working in the Academy.

My initial list of names for consideration began with eight women. I forwarded a letter and questionnaire to each person electronically via email, asking for a response within seven to ten days (See Appendix for the letter and list of questions). From the eight women, there were two rejections due to time constraints and other commitments. One person did not feel as qualified due to her short tenure in a leadership role, which I could respect. One participant selected, whom I conducted an initial interview with, left her position, and I was unable to conduct the final interview. Ultimately, the three women deans must be commended for "hanging in there" with me.

All three women are associate deans located at majority institutions. Two of the women are married and have children while the third is single and does not have any children. All names of the final participants have been kept confidential; pseudonyms have been used to identify them.

INTERVIEW PROCESS

Each interview was conducted at the participant's office. Knowing these women's position required them to conduct a lot of meetings and interact with a number of people on a day-to-day basis, our time spent together had to be limited. For the sake of privacy, time and space, they were kind enough to put their phones on hold and treat this interview with the utmost respect and treat me as their peer while we engaged in dialogue. On a few occasions, one of the participants may have had to take a call; however, this did not occur throughout the entire interview process.

RESEARCH DESIGN

The research design consisted of a three-part interview series. As noted by Seidman (1998) the interview process consisted of the following:

1. *Interview One: Focused Life History*—the participant's background was put into context asking about as much detail as possible which helped me as the researcher to become more familiar with the interviewee. In essence, the participant was asked to reconstruct their early experiences in their families, in school, with friends, their community, and workplace.
2. *Interview Two: The Details of the Experience*—this interview was focused on the concrete details of the participant's present experience and more specifically it got into the details of the topic area of the study. In order to put the participants' experience within the context of the social setting, the interviewee was asked to talk about her relationships with students, faculty, staff, and administrators and the wider community.
3. *Interview Three: Reflection on the Meaning*—the participants were asked to reflect more clearly on the meaning of their experience. "The question of 'meaning' is not one of satisfaction or reward . . . rather, it addresses the intellectual and emotional connections between the participants life and work."[17] Clearly, making sense or making meaning required the participants to look at how the factors in their lives interacted to bring them to their present situation. Hence, it required the participants' to look at their present experience in detail and within the context in which it occurred. "The combination of exploring the past to clarify the events that led participants to where they are now, and describing the concrete details of their present experience, establishes conditions for reflecting upon what they are now doing in their lives."[18]

Though this interview process consisted of a three-part series, I had to allow for some flexibility and combined part one and two in the first interview. Therefore, only two interviews were conducted of each participant instead of three. Seidman (1998) acknowledges that because inquiry is being done in order to learn about the complexities of which researchers are not totally aware, the design and even the focus of the study have to be seen as 'emergent' or "flexible."[19] By conducting the first and second part in the first interview, it allowed me to have the tapes transcribed and reflect on the third part, which focused on meaning-making. Condensing the number of interviews allowed for consideration of the participants' limited time constraints. At the same time, it allowed me to use the transcripts in a more meaningful way and get feedback through probing further and raising more insightful questions while having the participants respond directly to their initial comments from the first interview, which focused on their life history and details of their career.

The interview process took place over a period of nine months due to time constraints of the participants, location of participants and having to travel to their offices. Throughout the interview, with the permission of each participant, I used an audio-recorder and took field notes recording pertinent information that signified reexamination. After the interview process, I collected artifacts such as poetry, articles, and various other writings by each participant. According to LeCompte and Preissle (1993), the material recorded can include a variety of items such as: what investigators observe themselves, what they can induce participants to record, and what they and participants draw, photograph, tape record, film or videotape. In turn this creates a data bank of field notes, formal and informal interviews, questionnaires, written records, newspapers, memos, diaries, letters, recollections and reminiscences, myths, and folk tales.[20] In addition, material artifacts found on site, speeches, and books or articles written by the participants were included in this data bank.

Although I took field notes during the interview process, I heavily relied upon the audiotape so that I could listen intently and offer follow-up questions whenever necessary. After leaving each interview, I continued to add comments and considerations to think about as I reflected on the interview. The audiotapes were transcribed immediately after each interview, and I subsequently used a constant comparative method in extracting the emerging themes. Throughout the interview process and examining the transcripts, I was constantly looking for emerging and recurring themes, along with clarifying my own assumptions.

ANALYSIS

In analyzing and interpreting the data, I used a constant comparative method by looking at key words and phrases and emerging themes. I continuously looked at ways in which linkages of the data corresponded with proposed theoretical frameworks; yet, the experiences of these women are as critically important as theory itself. As a researcher, I was in correspondence with the participants via email or telephone to follow up with any additional questions regarding each interview. I also conducted a "member check" allowing the participants to review the data and how it has been recorded. After reviewing the data, I also allowed the participants to reflect and offer feedback on the information recorded to insure accuracy of the information provided.

Some considerations while analyzing and interpreting the data, included the following questions as outlined by Seidman (1998):

1. What connective threads are there among the experiences of the participants interviewed?
2. How does the researcher understand and explain these connections?
3. What does the researcher understand now that she did not understand before the interviews began?
4. What surprises occurred during the research process?
5. What confirmations of previous instincts?
6. How have the interviews been consistent with the literature?
7. How inconsistent?

After analyzing the data and reflecting on the above questions, it is clear that some of my initial instincts were confirmed while at the same time I encountered quite a few surprises, which will be discussed in Chapter Seven of this study.

CHAPTER 4
Flat-Footed Truths: Telling Black Women's Lives

> To tell the flat-footed truth means to offer a story or statement that is straightforward, unshakable, and unembellished. This kind of truth-telling, especially by and about Black women, can be risky business because our lives are often devalued and our voices periodically silenced. —Patricia Bell-Scott

FOR AFRICAN-AMERICAN WOMEN, THERE IS MUCH OF OUR STORY THAT has been left untold; yet, we have played a tremendous role in the building and strengthening of the fabric of American culture in many different ways. A short biographical representation of the women in this study will illuminate their lives, uncovering the silences of who they are and opening up a window of their lives to let their light shine through. These women's lives connect very much to my own experience in how I have and continue to encounter the world on a day-to-day basis, which includes the way I have chosen to negotiate spaces within the dominant culture. My spiritually guided walk through the Ivory Tower has allowed me to embrace those around me regardless of race, class, gender, ethnicity or any other type of difference and valuing the human spirit of individuals and hopefully finding a way to allow our spirits to connect. Yet, this has not always been a place of comfort because of various intrusions that have attempted to disrupt my way of knowing and being. While at the same time, it has been comforting to encounter individuals regardless of race, class, or gender who have connected with me as a genuine spirit and have maintained openness so that our spirits could grow together.

Often, the things we do as African-American women seem to go unnoticed or are recognized by only a few. Even in our busy day-to-day schedules, we forget our own accomplishments or the ways we have impacted other people's lives. For the most part, one's name, title, or position does not define who we are—it's the work we do which holds the most meaning and how we develop real and caring relationships with other human beings. While this may be the case for myself and the women in this study, not all women or people in influential leadership positions hold the same view. In the various discussions with Adjuoa, Chaka, and Jewel, it became clear to me that the status of their roles as deans was not the most important thing to them at the end of the day. Much of what has shaped their lives began with the foundation of their family upbringing, church, and communities where they grew up.

In the narratives of these women, we take a closer glimpse of my sisters and what's embedded in the fabric of their souls, and how they plant the seeds to nurture and influence others to develop to their fullest potential. Here, they relay their own "flat-footed truths."

ADJUOA

> This is my third class with her, and I remember I missed the first class of the first [course] I took with her that quarter, and when I came in the next week there were a few of us just mulling around, and I didn't know who she was, and I signed up for whatever the course name and description was at the time, and they said 'oh you'll know when she comes in the door even if you don't see her, you'll feel her in the room.' I thought, that's a really powerful statement to make about a professor, and I hadn't had that experience yet [at this university], and I thought ok . . . and you did . . . she is an energy . . . that is the reason I took this class. It wouldn't have mattered what it was titled. I needed energy this fall with everything that was going on, and I knew that no matter what was required in this course, the energy I would get from her would pull me through everything else.

No one had given me this type of heads up when I set out to find Adjuoa to participate in this study. Admittedly, one of Adjuoa's colleagues highly recommended her as a potential participant, though she never talked of her extensively. She just told me that we had some common interests in writing about spirituality and the two of us should connect. Yet, I find the student's statement to be quite true, because even in my first encounter with Adjuoa I felt she exuded a strong sense of presence, confidence, and spiritual wisdom.

On the day of our first meeting, I had a sense of nervous tension, especially since I had been waiting for almost a year to meet this woman. Indeed, the wait was more than worth it. The first words Adjuoa spoke when I walked into her office are still fresh in my mind. She said, "I said a prayer for you." *I thought to myself, I am glad you did because I needed it, and I prayed every step of the way to get to this office.* I graciously said, "Thank you," and sat down to calm my nerves and tell myself everything was going to be all right and it was going to be a great day. In the stillness of a few moments, a calming spirit and peace came over me despite the fact that I was approximately an hour late because I had turned off at the wrong exit, and it took me a while to get my bearings straight to get where I was supposed to be. I was more than anxious about this situation because I was concerned about time as a factor. Time is always of the essence, especially when asking someone else to share his/her time with you, and I didn't want Adjuoa to think that I was taking her time for granted. We ended up having more than enough time together, and she offered me the opportunity to attend her class and talk with her students about her.

Presence, confidence, and spiritual wisdom are words that symbolically embrace the full essence of Adjuoa's life and work. This tall, broadly built woman was dressed in a black, long, flowing wool dress adorned with an African mudcloth vest and black boots. Most fashionably, Adjuoa wore a loosely twisted dredlock hairstyle. Such characteristics reflecting her ethnic flavor clearly defy the traditional dress code or "norm" for women in leadership, particularly women in higher education located in a space called the "Ivory Tower." In our interview, Adjuoa confidently talked about her physical characteristics by saying, "I don't physically look like the other people on the dean's cabinet." She acknowledges there is another African-American on the deans' cabinet who is male, and his physical appearance folds into what may be considered more of the traditional dress for administrators in Academia. Adjuoa continued to talk about her physical presence and space by stating:

> I wear Africa as much in my body as I do in the things I think about and the way that I feel, and I embrace it in the outward appearance as well. So, I don't physically look like. . . don't put myself together in the traditional way of a Dean or an Associate Dean.

Oddly enough, African Americans have to justify or continuously clarify to others what their African-centered dress or hairstyles represent, while most people from other ethnic groups are left to maintain their situated identity and physical presence in whatever space they are in. For example, ethnic groups from India or various other Asian countries who wear traditional dress are identified from their cultural and ethnic frame of reference without having to justify their "beingness." In America this holds true for Appalachian, Amish, Native Americans and other groups of people who are culturally centered; yet, African Americans continuously have to justify what their beingness means in physical spaces wherever we go. Clearly, Adjuoa's spiritual beingness woven together with her physical presence helps to serve as a buffer when others may question her situated identity. In essence, her own identity politics does not allow other people who may question or be curious of her physical characteristics to disrupt her sense of being.

Growing up in a large city located in the Northwest of the United States provided Adjuoa with a rich multicultural experience. Though I mistakenly thought a woman of her age group would have grown up in a predominantly black community, I soon realized that my thinking was totally wrong. Adjuoa grew up in a multicultural community broadly defined by many different ethnic groups. As she described it,

> I grew up with all different kinds of people speaking all different kinds of languages. So I've always lived in the world . . . The schools I went to . . .they were sort of equally balanced so you had equal numbers, or at least more equal than here, numbers of African Americans, European Americans, a large Asian-American population, growing Latino population and then some folks just came from everywhere. So, I grew up eating with chop sticks . . . [For lunch] I'd trade off my peanut butter and jelly for somebody else's rice and teriyaki. So, I grew up with that, and I don't know a community like a lot of black folks have constructed community to just mean black people. When Mrs. Chow up the street chastised us and she did it in Chinese, we didn't understand; we knew we were in trouble and she was going to figure out whatever little bit of English she could to go tell my mother about what we had done. The same thing was true with Mrs. Garcia . . . So that is the community I grew up in.

As Adjuoa alluded, the notion of community resonates quite differently for many African Americans in the United States. Even today, African Americans are demographically located in segregated pockets, both urban, suburban and rural, throughout the country; however, there are many others who have branched out beyond borders to communities that do not traditionally reflect a predominant sector of African Americans. Though there are many reasons today why African Americans live in nontraditional communities, one factor attributing to such changes is the social and economic gains African Americans have made during the last twenty-five to thirty years.

For Adjuoa, not only has growing up in a multicultural community played a significant role in her life, it has also heavily influenced how she broadly defines community and where she does her work. Community thus extends beyond the university where she serves as an administrator and teacher, and/or where she lives. Community for Adjuoa extends beyond the borders of the United States to where she has built a school in Ghana, West Africa. She also plans to build more schools in the village where she was recently named a chief.

Although Adjuoa's cultural community was broadly defined early on in life, there was still one sector that was predominantly black—the African-American church she grew up in. Adjuoa and her family *"lived in the church,"* her father was a deacon and her mother was extensively involved in different church groups. When Adjuoa and her four siblings were in high school they were given the option to attend church. As she shared with me, most of them opted out of attending church; however, it did not stop her own spiritual growth and development.

Though Adjuoa's family and church had an impact on her spiritual development while growing up, it is clear that she does not couch her own meaning of spirituality according to religious dogma. When asked how she makes meaning of her spirituality, she defined it in this way:

> It means listening to and being talked to by whomever you consider your higher being, your highest self and being influenced by the voices of your highest self. But for me, spirituality is all about both talking and listening. It's difficult, I think, to be a spiritual person if one isn't constantly in prayer or in quiet creating all sorts of sacred spaces to listen, but it's also very critical for me in terms of thinking about spirituality that there is a sense of action, and action may be solely that of speech, but being spiritual or recognizing spirituality in my life also means that I work, I do something as a result of having heard what my highest voice says, that moves beyond just me.

Clearly, Adjuoa's early life lessons were influenced heavily by her family. Her interest in becoming a teacher was influenced heavily by her father who was a teacher, though her mother taught her plenty of life lessons on what it meant to be a woman in our society. Adjuoa also notes her mother was instrumental in her life and encouraging her to do whatever she wanted to do in life. Adjuoa stated:

> She was always there to say go . . .you want to go hiking, go. If you want to go canoeing, go do it. You want to be a writer, fine. You want to go off to college somewhere where we don't know where it is, fine. You're going off to El Salvador, fine. She wasn't as fine with that as a lot of others, but she knew she couldn't say no to me and didn't ask me to make the kind of choices between what traditionally being a woman meant and the way I was constructing woman, especially African-American women. So my mother has been critical. My mother continues to be critical in that role.

Another person who influenced Adjuoa's interest in becoming a teacher was her kindergarten teacher who was the only African-American teacher she had throughout her K-12 experience. When we talked about other influential role models, Adjuoa stated, " . . . This woman had an amazing voice, and she was a very creative sister . . . she also was exciting to me. I wanted to be like Mrs. Jones, and so she was an important [role] model." In addition, there have been other people (non African-American) in teaching and administration who have served as mentors or guides throughout her educational experience and career path.

During the time of this interview, Adjuoa served as an Associate Dean of a large university. Since Fall 2001, she has returned to leading in the classroom full-time and "moving hearts, minds, and souls" in that particular space. Adjuoa admits that serving as an administrator is something she is comfortable doing. However, she confesses that teaching is her first love.

JEWEL

On the day I met Jewel, I had presented the testimonial "My Soul Looks Back and Wonders How I Got Over" about my grandmother's influence on my life earlier that day, so I was already riding on a natural high. Prior to our scheduled interview, I was invited to listen to Jewel give a discussion on her new book with a group of mostly undergraduate students taking a Women's Studies course. Jewel's book was one of the required readings for this course.

The class discussion that evening was held at a lodge. In this log cabin, the warmth of a fireplace created quite a cozy and intimate setting for all of us. This was a time when both students and faculty could really let their hair down, relax and enjoy having the author describe what her work was all about. Jewel had just published a book on African-American women writers of the late eighteenth and early nineteenth century. I sat in on the gathering listening intently to Jewel's soft-spoken voice as she shared with students how she came to know and write about the women in her work. Beforehand, Jewel shared ideas about herself as a writer and her own situated identity:

> Introspection permits you to have agency in your own life, it permits you to take on the kind of persona you want to create to be bold enough to be flexible and say who you want to be.

Jewel continued to share with us the situated identity of the women she wrote about in her work by stating:

> Historically, looking at African-American women there's a certain type of consciousness no matter what type of writings African-American women create. Underneath what the author said there was an ideology operating . . . sending messages down through the generations. African-American women wrote with rhetorical purpose. They didn't

always write things one way so that you can get it [the message], they wrote in different ways. African-American women wrote across genres.

Formally, Jewel's educational training is in linguistics, and she said that this particular work offers three distinct perspectives, which include the rhetorical, historical, and ideological. By creating this work in this way, it allows Jewel to look for patterns and to determine who is doing what and analyze these women's lives and their way of life in this way. Jewel commented that there is a "sense of liberation when you tinker." According to Jewel, the tinkering allows one to structure him/herself in doing the type of writing she does. Jewel then raised several rhetorical questions for students to think about such as, *"What kind of faith do you have in your own vision, what would make you think that you have something interesting enough to write about that others would be interested in?"*

Finally, Jewel commented specifically on one of the nineteenth century women in her book by stating, *"People talk about Sojourner Truth as an illiterate person . . . it was almost important to be illiterate in a literate environment during her time."* Jewel then raised this question to the audience, *"What type of literacy did she have?"* Jewel answered by saying, *"From a socio-cognitive perspective, Sojourner Truth was smart enough and bold enough to tell people about themselves. She read the situation, she read the man, she called him and told him about himself."* This short synopsis of the gathering that evening only provides a portion of the thought and ideas Jewel left on the minds of these undergraduate students who were attempting to make sense of their own work and how they write and read other works by important scholars.

After the book discussion and reception that evening, I was somewhat concerned about whether Jewel would still feel up to an interview with me, since she had already given an hour-long book discussion. I asked her, and she gladly responded in the affirmative.

I drove Jewel to her hotel where we held the formal interview. Jewel took her shoes off and told me to make myself comfortable. Instead of sitting in chairs at a table, Jewel reclined on one of the beds while I took her advice and made myself comfortable sitting on the other bed in a yoga posture. Like the other women in this study, Jewel was recommended to me by another administrator in higher education. After I forwarded her a letter and questionnaire about the subject matter, Jewel willingly agreed to accept the participant role. Though she warned me of her tight schedule, we managed to get our interviews completed in a timely manner.

By cultural and geographical standards, Jewel would be labeled as a "Southern Belle," a name that some women of the South carry with great pride. Reared as an only child within a close-knit family, Jewel grew up with her parents in a small southern town. Jewel commented about her social and cultural ways of knowing and learning about the world early on in her life by saying, "*I was one of those people who was kind of raised to serve the community of which I was a part, and much of what I have done has been a part of that ethos.*" When asked about what influenced her to pursue a career in higher education, she first made it clear that she didn't have a choice in the pursuit of education. Jewel responded by saying:

> I grew up in a family that valued education deeply, and so the expectation was that I would go on until I decided to stop and I just never stopped . . . I did teach elementary school for a year, and again that wasn't because I was geared toward elementary school. It was a job in my hometown, and I was raised to give back to the community.

Jewel learned from this teaching experience that she liked to teach, but teaching on the elementary school level wasn't for her. Jewel admitted that after obtaining her undergraduate degree her educational path was not clear-cut, and some things kind of fell into her lap. Basically, the opportunity presented itself for her to pursue the next degree, and that's what she did. She acknowledged this by saying, "I haven't been at all goal-oriented in my choices." As the old cliché goes, "one thing came after the other," which is how Jewel ended up on a career track in higher education. Once again, she acknowledged that even in her faculty teaching experience she had not set out to pursue a leadership role though she has served in many. Even the current position as an associate dean is not a leadership role she set out to obtain. She was asked by the Dean to consider the position.

When Jewel was asked to respond about some of the women who influenced her education and career endeavors, she responded:

> There have been many women who have influenced my life whom I value deeply for the lives that they've led. Because my career choice hasn't been particularly goal oriented, I haven't had people that have necessarily influenced me to do this work. I've had people who have influenced me to do whatever I do well. I have had people who have influenced me to value my academic abilities. What I call the most unforgettable character in my life is my mother. She's just incredible. She's still living, and she was a rural schoolteacher, and I do admire her and the life she led, the way that she led, and the values and principles that she lives by.

In many ways, Jewel's ethos carries much of the wisdom that was imparted by her mother. She commented further on these values by stating:

> She believes that anything worth doing is worth doing well. That's kind of basic, and she believes in leading a life that makes the difference. In essence, if you have had a life, it should have made a difference to

> somebody. That's the way that she's living life and how I have learned to live mine. If nobody knows that you've been here, you've wasted your time. I did not want to do what she did. She was a rural school teacher, and I didn't want that life. But I have always been grateful that she did it and showed it to me in that way.
>
> She had a particular commitment that she believed in being active at church. She believed in being active in her community. She believed in being active in her school. So anywhere she was, she was going to be active. And I find it hard not to do that. If you're going to be there you need to be doing something. So it's those kinds of values that are clearly the values that I live by. She believes in honesty. She believes in integrity. As a friend of mine likes to say about her, she does not suffer fools well. That kind of thing. And of course I grew up around women like her. Not all educated women or anything but women who were strong and who led good lives and took care of their families and were active in their communities and did meaningful things for the lives of the people around them. So collectively they are who I am. Beyond that, the women that I've been most inspired by have been the women I've studied.

The way Jewel humbly talks about her mother's wisdom very much resonates in her own life and how she talks about leadership. Jewel modestly shared her perspective on leadership and how she perceives herself as a leader by saying:

> I don't think of myself as leading much. I think of myself as a facilitator of things and as an enabler of things. I'm not one who particularly likes being out front or controlling other people. I'd rather see things emerge. I'd rather witness growth . . . that kind of thing. That tends to be the style I have. I'm not particularly competitive though I like to be the best. The best for me is internally driven, not externally driven. So it doesn't bother me that someone else could also be the best. And so leadership to me is most evident in what the women I studied make central in their lives and that people who are able to make the world a better place in whatever way they manage to do that. Other kinds of leadership to me are other things that people call leadership, which are about other things [related to their own agenda]. I guess in my definition of leadership what matters is the one that helps the world be better.

In addition to describing her leadership as a facilitator, she also described her work as "serving" in order to make a difference in other people's lives. In many ways, these ideas parallel the way Jewel talks about her spiritual life. When asked how she describes spirituality and what it means to her life, she responded:

> I don't tie spirituality and religion together. I think that human beings have spiritual dimensions. The things that are accounted for dynamically in that relationship between the heart and mind, and I talk about dimensions like that completely as heart, mind, spirit, and backbone, (but the categories aren't quite in that [distinct] way of talking about dimensions of the body). That is much of what I mean when I say that I like to keep myself in balance in a significant way, [and] those are the important things in keeping in balance. In other words I do believe that the soul should be fed, it should be nourished. People need to feel loved and cared for. They need to feel there's meaning in life. They need to feel anchored in a positive way to the universe. Now, a lot of people talk about those things in religious terms. I grew up with those kinds of terms, but my sense of spirituality is not tied to those kinds of terms anymore. I don't know if they ever were as such, but certainly what that desired goal is for is also what I value.

Jewel then says that she feeds her soul in various ways, such as:

> With people and my relationships with them, introspection and my relationship with myself, with reflection, with music and art, the beauty of the world, the things that let me know that there is, for lack of a better term, without a shadow of a doubt there is something bigger than an individual self. Whether that's a collectivity of all of us as human beings . . . I don't try to name that. I just know there's something bigger than us.

Jewel continues this dialogue on spirituality by stating:

> Some people frame it in terms of a higher being. Some people frame it in terms of a soul or kind of a God of the universe. Whatever it is, of all things, I accept that as a possibility. What I know in my own mind is that I feel that the dynamism of living in a way that was not my making. Maybe that's the way to say it. So even if it's just a hope, I hope that that's not my imagination. And I believe that, to use traditional terms, I have been blessed in a way that lets me know that I don't take credit for the dynamism.

While sitting in the book discussion, Jewel mentioned the idea of faith in her work. Therefore, I asked her to talk more explicitly about what faith means to her. She replied:

> In the most mundane terms, faith and belief are words that are used relatively interchangeably, and again, they are not always tied to religion in the way people traditionally by default [talk about it]. So I'm not invoking the name of the Lord Jesus or God Almighty or anything like that . . . though I don't have any problem with doing that. When I

> talk about faith and belief in the most mundane way, I think that there is power in the universe and that power is ultimately directed toward good. I think that the good is balance and harmony and that the world balances and harmonizes itself in the same way that I try to do my own life. And with a belief in goodness, balance, and harmony I don't worry about the evil that men do. Again, to invoke those kinds of traditional, religious tones, I believe that the power of belief in goodness is the power that sustains me. And so when I talk about faith, and I was talking about it today, you have to have faith that the move that you make as a writer, even though it may be a high-risk move, is worth the effort. And to me that says that you don't have to worry about retribution. You don't have to worry so much about how people are going to perceive that if you have been thoughtful and reflective about the truth . . . your truth . . . your authenticity . . . your honesty in whatever it is that you're saying and doing. So it's a double-edged sword in that sense that to the extent that you can feel that you've done your own internal work then your actions stand for whatever they stand for and what I've tried to live toward is to be comfortable with standing by my actions in that way.

In fully tying together how Jewel thinks about spirituality, she comments:

> I don't think I have a neat definition of spirituality or one that I wouldn't want to change with the next sentence, but certainly I think it's accurate to say that I think there is personal power in the spirituality that I'm talking about. I think that there is collective power in the spirituality that I'm talking about. I think that there is energy. I think there is synergy . . . again matching up personal and collective energy and synergy. And I think that engagement with, for a lack of other terms, with the deep places in ourselves is empowering.

CHAKA

I met Chaka during my first year of graduate school. We became more acquainted at the end of that first year when I learned of changes that would be taking place in the office where I was working. I decided to be bold enough to approach Chaka and ask her if she needed a graduate assistant for the following year. I quickly described to her my academic and student affairs background hoping that something I said would be seen as a match. The two of us talked briefly, and by the end of the conversation we felt as if "kindred spirits" were being connected. I needed a new home and Chaka needed some help in an area where I had experience, so I couldn't ask for more. After our meeting, I walked away thinking to myself, "Thank God, I have a new home." This relationship extended beyond our working together on special programs—Chaka and I had an opportunity to teach together, and she became one of the best mentors for me during my graduate program.

Chaka spent most of her adolescent and adult life in the Midwest with her parents and three sisters. Interestingly, Chaka's father was a minister, yet he helped her to understand and frame spirituality beyond the boundaries of religious dogma. Chaka admits that some of the core tenets of her faith come from the Black church, however, she frames her spirituality and how she was influenced quite differently from a religious sect or symbolic notions of a particular denomination. Chaka made this clear by stating:

> I learned a lot of my faith-based beliefs in the context of the historically African-American church, with my father being a minister. I think the advantage of his being a minister was what that afforded me as he helped us separate the human-constructed organization from the core spiritual and theologically-based beliefs. And I remember so distinctly asking him questions about why we have to wear dresses to church and he says, 'You don't.' And back in the old days women wore hats, and he says, 'You don't.' That's all made up . . . human beings made that all up. And I tell him now I appreciate that so much, and I said, what would you do if I wore pants to church and he says, 'Nothing, you wear pants, you wear pants. I'll tell you what will happen. People might say something, but God isn't going to look at you any differently.' So it just really blew me away. So I think both he and my mom were very progressive, especially for that time, and we went to Catholic schools and we were not Catholic.

In talking more about the influence of the community and the black church, Chaka indicated:

> I think the experience I had being in a predominantly Black neighborhood is so distinctly different from what many Black kids have today. Where you get that natural validation every second of your life, either from the teacher or from "Ms. So and So" next door. So, I think it's real critical that those of us who feel that a part of our calling is working with youth, I think the church is important. Because a lot of kids, Black kids today, don't get that natural validation, not in their school and not in their neighborhood. So the only, the last place for them to get it is at church. So, what's so critically important [today] and where the extension of our work has meaning, is by exercising [it] in a church with young people.

Chaka further discusses her spirituality by saying:

> My whole spiritual nature is very much connected in a supreme being, not in human beings being the end all . . . not in the trees being the end

> all even though I respect everyone else's right to believe or worship and be guided by whatever they choose. But for me, very clearly, there is something much greater and powerful and more infinite than human beings and the metaphysical stuff that we see around us. So, it's really a belief in that supreme being whose essence is one of holiness with total positive regard for us and always wanting us to aspire to be like that being.

She continues by stating:

> This spirituality gives me meaning, keeps me grounded, gives me a sense of purpose, and quite frankly helps me laugh at the things that happen in this world because I know that there are some things so trivial in the larger scheme of things and sometimes I think as a human being it's hard to remember that.

Chaka also noted that her spirituality means that "there is a divine purpose for why [she's] here at this moment, and if [she] can remain connected to that purpose then all the junk that's thrown [her] way pales." In essence, Chaka sees her spirituality as keeping her centered, giving her meaning, and guiding her actions.

Chaka's parents hold much credit for her educational pursuit. This was made clear when she stated:

> I was always in an environment where education was almost the centerpiece of our family life because both of my parents are educators. And so that was just a huge theme in my early years . . . . They instilled in us, though, a love for learning, and there was no question we were going to college, and there was no question that we were going to pursue the highest degree we could or should or needed for our career choices. I think my parents both modeled for us that learning was a lifelong venture.

Not only were Chaka's parents influential in her education, but she also had two African-American professors during her undergraduate experience who helped crystallize her interest in becoming a psychologist. This was evident when Chaka spoke of these professors:

> I was fortunate when I went to the University to have an African-American professor who just, I think, absolutely put everything in place for me, he and his wife. Both were so instrumental that I always tell them, you're the reason I became a psychologist. They kind of clarified the path for me even though I kind of knew generally what I needed to do. They also made it seem like a reachable goal, and by reachable I mean I always thought I had the capability, but some things,

> especially when you're at a predominantly White university, it's not so clear, at least for me. What if I don't get into a doctoral program or what if this stuff doesn't happen the way I want it to happen. So they really supported me and really said, 'You have what it takes and don't ever give up . . . here's what you do.' Then, they also modeled for me how all this was possible because they were professors.

Not surprisingly, there have been several women in Chaka's life who have influenced her educational and career endeavors. However, the one woman who stands out the most in influencing her leadership and how she has constructed her identity is her mother. With pride, Chaka shares her response to the question:

> Believe it or not, my mom. Even though a lot of people say she wasn't a leader like the principal of a school or anything like that, but she was a leader in her classroom, and as a parent we're leaders and sometimes . . . it's funny . . . I just saw my mom last weekend, and I had her cracking up because I said, mom you just don't know how often I think about how you would handle situations with us . . . . So she modeled I think the way to really deal with difficult situations by basically having the person just prove to themselves that what they just said was the most asinine thing that they ever could have asked and they knew better . . . like do not waste my time . . . because you know this is not going to happen . . . I think she was a good mediator . . . conflict mediator.

When talking about how her family or other people perceived Chaka, she responded:

> I'm speaking of my sisters and parents because my kids they would say, 'Oh she's mom, she's nice, she can be mean . . . but she loves us.' So they would say things like that. My sisters and my parents would say . . . because I think that they view me now more [outside of my leadership] role. I think my children view me in my role. [My sisters and parents] view me as a whole person. They would say, 'Chaka is very focused. She's sensitive. She's humorous and fun loving. I think they'd say she's very kind. She can be very direct, though, and will not mince words.' I think they'd say 'She stands her ground,' and I know my husband would definitely say this. Sometimes in a stubborn way and that is true. If I really feel that this is the right thing I will not budge. If I have doubts, then I'll leave the room for a moment. And a good listener. Those kinds of things. And I think my oldest daughter would concur with that because she's getting to an age now where she sees me as more than just a mom. We were talking the other night, and she just told me that she hopes that she can be as focused a person as I am . . . she didn't use the word focus . . . what word did she use? She said,

> 'Mom you stay on track with things' . . . something like that because we were talking about looking at colleges and career options and things. So I think she would say that, but my other two children just see me as a mom . . . even my son tells me, 'Mom, sometimes you just' . . . I just what? 'See, there you go!' I don't know what he's talking about.

In listening to Adjuoa, Jewel, and Chaka, it reminded me of quilting together so many African-American women's stories whose lives have been so full of vibrancy and color. The way these women talk about their spirituality and how they make meaning of their lives through leadership comes together more fully in Chapter Five. The way Adjuoa, Jewel and Chaka talked about their leadership revealed several themes, which helped me better understand how they make sense of self and their mission and purpose in life. These themes will be fully explicated in the next chapter, which further illuminates how their spirituality is inextricably woven into their leadership and how they make meaning of their lives.

CHAPTER 5

The Soul of My Sisters: Talkin' and Testifyin'

> My work is to inhabit the silences with which I have lived and fill them with myself until they have the sounds of brightest day and the loudest thunder.—Audre Lorde

EVERY TIME AFRICAN-AMERICAN WOMEN TALK ABOUT THEIR LIVES, IT pushes back the silences of the unknown, which has typically forecasted our lives into stereotypical fashions or objectified our lives as the exotic. Adjuoa, Chaka and Jewel share their life stories, bringing forth the "truths" of their own spiritual foundation and how they arrived at where they are today. Their life stories convey their experience serving as deans at majority institutions. In listening to these women's stories, they have continued to convey who they are, their sense of mission and purpose in life, and how they make personal meaning of their work acknowledging that there is a power greater than one's self.

Several themes emerged that speak to Adjuoa's, Chaka's, and Jewel's spiritually guided leadership. First, naming and knowing self according to one's own standpoint very much addresses how these women understand their sense of self, mission, and purpose in life. In essence, the titles these women hold does not make them who they are, instead, it gives them credit for their role. Second, providing and maintaining an ethic of care through mentoring, "mothering, and othermothering," is central to these women's strong sense of self and how they make personal meaning of their work. Third, leadership for social justice is inextricably woven into the everyday practices of how these women carry out their work; their conveying a moral ethic, a moral and ethical standard of values and principles, which keeps them from wavering in their leadership practices. Fourth, these women's life work extends far beyond the Academy, which very much resonates with the long held tradition of African Americans "giving back" to their communities. In this case, however, community is broadly defined, and how these women talk about their communities has been resituated or redefined unlike what one would have thought of as community thirty to forty years ago. Today, their activism can be defined in a way that moves them to pushing borders and crossing boundaries in their everyday work.

THEME ONE: SPIRITUALLY GUIDED LEADERSHIP THROUGH SERVANTHOOD

The African-American women in this study elucidate the phenomenon of servanthood in their narratives when discussing their leadership and work both within Academia and beyond. In these narratives, one finds that the way these women administrators talk about their leadership and how they work with other individuals has less to do with their own self-interests and focuses more on serving others. This type of servanthood characteristically embodies recognizing that their purpose in life has a greater meaning far beyond themselves. In essence, the recognition of a title is less important than the work they have committed themselves to do.

One participant, Adjuoa, described her work to the extent of not being "vested in the role of Associate Dean or Assistant Dean"; however, she described her work as having a greater purpose. She stated:

> I am led by something beyond that [role] and have a purpose for this work . . . . I would say that about my teaching role and any other attached role or title that someone would give me. I work beyond that. There's a purpose beyond that.

When I asked Adjuoa what that purpose is, she responded:

> It takes us back to something you asked earlier. It's about opening up opportunities for people to be their best selves. That is the purpose. It's about creating spaces of peace in the world and walking in love.

In the same vein, Fairholm (1997) offers and supports this idea by stating, "Power, wealth and prestige are not definitive of spiritual leaders. Rather, the transcendent values of spiritual leaders include a rejection of self-interest and a focus on servanthood."[1] When talking with Adjuoa, this became evident in the way she leads her life and the relationships she has with others. First, I asked her to describe how her leadership may be different from traditional ways of leadership in the Academy, and she responded in this way:

> The first thing that popped in my head, and this is why I'm giggling, is ego . . . I'm not wrapped up in it. They're wrapped up in the status of the position. Singular . . . maybe solo but done as an individual versus somehow collaborative ways or more fruitful ways . . . there's a sort of sameness . . . a desire to be like everyone else . . . so a buy-in, if you will, to what administration means. So in some ways a lot of other folks have a common understanding of what leadership means, and they work within the frame of that common understanding and I'm not interested in the common understanding. Maybe I don't even know the common understanding, but it doesn't fit very well with me.

Adjuoa adds:

> I think, rather than mechanistic, [the leadership] is more standardized . . . There's a standard by which we understand, by which we know what a leader is, and it's that standard that I don't choose to engage. I don't choose to engage leadership in that way. I don't think that's what's called for right now, and I say that across racial and ethnic groups. I just don't think it's what we need, and it's loveless.

Adjuoa also finds it very important to maintain congruence in her leadership, by not just "talking the talk, but walking the walk." She acknowledges this by saying:

> I talk a lot about congruence in the classes that I teach because I think teachers are often very incongruent so that what we would see, for example, in their behavior at home and their behavior at the bar with their friends and the behavior in the classrooms and their behavior as graduate students here are very different people. I seek congruence and I think one of the major differences between myself as a leader and between others as leaders is that there is a seeking of congruence. If I have to be "X" and be "X" in one context, that's fine. And then I'll be a different "X" over there. So we never quite know which leader we're dealing with, and I'm much more interested in being me . . . how I am here, there and everywhere so that people come to know what to expect from me or of me as me.

In another way, Jewel's spiritually guided leadership stems from being raised in a community where she was taught to be of service. "I was raised to serve the community of which I was a part, and much of what I have done has been a part of that ethos," says Jewel. In describing her leadership style, Jewel humbly responded:

> I don't think of myself as leading much. I think of myself as a facilitator of things and as an enabler of things. I'm not one who particularly

> likes being out front or controlling other people. I'd rather see things emerge. I'd rather witness growth.

Interestingly, this perspective was confirmed at another point in our interview by the way Jewel talked about a program she developed while working at another university:

> It's not that I feel that I take personal credit . . . oh look what I did, but it's more that I feel that I was able to enable certain paths of things, to facilitate certain kinds of things by that work, and I'm affirmed by the fact that that work is ongoing without me because I'm no longer there. [I] haven't been there in a good while, but I'm still there.

Though Jewel has recently published a book about African-American women writers of the nineteenth century, she's quite modest about how she would like to be remembered. Here's a part of that dialogue:

R: When the last chapter is written in your autobiography, what would you want people to know about you?

J: That's an interesting question for me because I would probably be one of those people that would still want people to be wondering who I was. I don't want them to know too much about me.

R: So you wouldn't want people to know very much about you?

J: Well, I would hope they would say that I was very good at what I did. And that I was a good person as well as good at work. I like the notion of being honest and fair and forthright . . . those kind of characteristics. And I believe that's what people would say.

Despite Jewel's own modesty in how she talks about her leadership and work, it becomes clearer that she is less concerned with the title or titles that she hold, but more interested in the way she serves others.

After examining the stories of the other two participants, it should not come as a surprise that Chaka's words resonate with this theme of servanthood as she talks about her life and how she makes meaning of her leadership:

> Whenever I think of that word [meaning leadership], the first word that always come to my mind, and it's probably not one that most people think of, but being a servant comes up for me a lot. As a theme, I think that's a big part of it. Most people first think about power, think about control, think about vision. And all of those things are a part of leadership, but the overriding theme for me . . . I think the ultimate leader is the person who can serve the people. Now, that service means

> facilitating the needs of the people being met, organization, whatever it is you're leading . . . it depends on the context, but facilitating the needs of the students being met or the needs of the country being met, or the needs of the church being met . . . whatever. And that can only be done, obviously, by knowing your skill set, by knowing the needs of the people, by being able to craft the vision and facilitate the vision no matter how you come up with it by a kind of leveraging all of the talents in the organization. I mean, there's all that stuff that has to happen with it. And of course, with that comes some amount of power, but I think I tend not to focus on the power part, on the control part, and focus a lot more just on facilitating the needs of the organization or group being met and moving it in the direction that has been crafted for it. So, for me, that's what I tend to think about, and I think it takes someone who sees themselves as the servant for the group to make that happen.

Chaka's response to the question, "In what ways has spirituality played a role in shaping who you are as a leader?" was:

> I think it's given me a road map and a guide. When I say road map and a guide, it's how to be with other people and how to make decisions. And as I mentioned before, it's really helped me to cope because it's been a reminder that this is just really not that important . . . this does not define who I am, and so I think that's the trap leaders get into with the whole power thing. It's like, when that defines who you are, then those decisions become real high-stake decisions because it's like protecting your own ego. You're not connected with something beyond this. This is reality for you . . . this role or this world, so therefore it begins to feed your own selfish kind of agenda as opposed to really being grounded in something that's beyond that.

THEME TWO: A CALL TO CONSCIOUSNESS IN EVERYDAY PRACTICE: EXERCISING AN ETHIC OF CARE

Talking with the heart taps the ethic of caring, which serves as another dimension of an alternative epistemology used by African-American women. As noted by Collins (2000) there are three inter-related components of the ethic of caring which include: (1) the value placed on individual uniqueness/expressiveness, (2) the appropriateness of emotions, and (3) the capacity for empathy,[2] which will be elucidated in the following section.

By developing and maintaining an ethic of care, African-American women in the Academy have served as buffers, catalysts for change, and pillars of strength through mentoring, "othermothering," and creating and opening spaces for traditionally marginalized groups of people.

Chaka communicates many of her values by the way she discusses what's most important in her role as an administrator, which is keeping at the forefront the idea of "reminding ourselves of why we are here." In turn, this translates into how she makes daily connections with other administrators, faculty and students. Chaka states:

> What's neat about being in the position I'm in, even though I may not work with students directly, I can not leave my office and walk down the hall without seeing a student . . . so, students are the visible reminder for me. So, that's why I'm here, that helps. And of course, I also teach, which is one of the reasons why I still teach, even though it's just one class a year, but it's also to keep me grounded and [to know] this is the reason why I'm here.

Chaka's sense of care can be understood by the way she talks about "impacting the system." Here she states:

> What I like most is being able to impact the system in which students can thrive . . . Impacting the system means making sure that the structure of this institution is one where students have the flexibility to really grow by exploring what they need to explore. That's different for every student, but certainly having access to experiences where they can learn, having access to seasoned scholars or those who have gone through learning as part of their education who can support them in that. And, what does that look like?

Chaka continues:

> Well, it looks like a place where you have a broad curriculum that reflects the diversity of knowledge that's out there. That is, everyone changing to some extent . . . you know, knowledge, we've got to keep up with all of that. But, also it respects the historical grounding that knowledge is built upon and has a diverse array of voices at the learning table. That's kind of what it looks like so that those rich discussions can occur.

In another way, Chaka's embodiment of an ethic of care in her work offers meaning when she talks about how she would envision herself being remembered by others:

> It's important for me to do that [put others first] because I think that's really at the center of my life's work: to empower others and I think as a clinician you do that. You can't be selfish . . . you can't want to be the focus of attention. You can't always want the spotlight to be on you . . . I never conceptualize myself being at the center. I always conceptualize the student and their quest for knowledge being the center, and

> I'm there as kind of like the cheerleader for them or the person who is really trying to help them struggle through the issues. So I try to keep myself out of the center of their work but be there to facilitate their work. And the same thing is true in my role as an administrator where a lot of people look at it as the whole power trip thing, and I don't look at it that way at all, and I try a lot to kind of keep out of the way. So, in all aspects of my career, and really in my personal life . . . I've made career decisions not necessarily on what was best for me because my career advancement was based upon what was best for my family. Because if I hadn't, I would not be here at this [university] at this time. I'd be at another university in a position that had slightly more money and a little more autonomy, but it wasn't best for my family. So, I think that theme has kind of guided a lot of my decisions.

When talking about mentoring, this is not a subject that is taken lightly by any of the women in this study. Adjuoa made this clear when she talked about her mentoring experience as a doctoral student and how her advisor modeled in a way that has influenced how she attempts to serve as a mentor. Adjuoa says:

> My dissertation advisor is the personification of a mentor. I might have been the only African American he ever knew, and he didn't know my subjects . . . he didn't know what I was studying. He didn't know much about culture, but he cared about race. He didn't know a lot about being a [woman], but he cared about me. And, when I think about how I advise my doc students, how I teach, how I try to support them once they leave me . . . I think about his model . . . the way he did that for me is how I attempt to do that for my students.

Adjuoa continued to proudly talk about the role her advisor has played and continues to play in her life. She commented that he still attends presentations she gives at conferences, and he still asks her to write [for publication] or present [at conferences] together with him.

For many students who have had an encounter with Adjuoa through coursework, it is clear that she has exemplified being a mentor and role model for her students. Unquestionably, there are some students who acknowledged that she has had a significant impact on their lives. It was quite an awestruck moment for me to step into Adjuoa's classroom unannounced and ask graduate students about her role as a professor and how they make meaning of their encounter with her. Here are some of the student comments,

> Student #1: I can put her in so many perspectives . . . I can put her as a thought . . . she's that thought that will make you smile . . . like a son doing good for his mother . . . she creates a space where I want to be

so good at everything that I do in her class for her, but I know that by being the best that I can be as a student in her class, I am becoming better as a person, as a student, as an educator, as an African-American male, but she really makes me want to do something . . . she makes me want to challenge who I am and challenge what I am good at as a student and as a professional. She is a powerful force, a happy, powerful force that takes me back to when I was an adolescent. As a child in kindergarten you're a sponge ready to absorb all this knowledge, and you're excited to learn something because you know you're going to get something and this is the place to get it. She makes [me] feel comfortable that I'm going to get something either I didn't expect and/or everything she said I was going to get and more. She is a great, great individual for me.

Student #2: This is my third class with her, and the biggest thing that I've recognized, and I even took a spirituality class with her, is that spirituality guides her life. It's everywhere a part of her. She teaches it. She actually writes it in her own journals, and she actually uses those kinds of comments lots of times in her journal. So I think as a mentor she's a good person to strive for your spirituality. And another thing that I've noticed is that she makes you responsible for your own learning. She wants you to accept responsibility for your learning. She wants you to push yourself and do things you're not used to doing but, she also creates that space that's safe enough to do it. Because if you don't feel comfortable enough, you're not going to explore, and I guess those are the three things that I can say that are wonderful about her . . . that I really appreciate and wish every other teacher had some aspects of those in some depth because she has tremendous depth.

Student #3: As with the others, I also had an in-depth relationship with [Adjuoa] and one of the unique things about her that I would say first struck me was she was one of the few professors who I've encountered who actually spoke of doing their work for a higher purpose and one of the questions that she often posed to myself in things I'm struggling through right now is that, for whom do you actually do your work? And she was one of the only people I encountered who sort of makes it her purpose to do her work for the Creator. Everything that she does, her pedagogy, the way she teaches, her research, everything is dedicated toward a higher being and for me that was an eye opener because particularly at a place like this [where] the kinds of things I'm hearing [are] tenure, research creating new avenues, whereas she says all of her work is in the area of producing things for the Creator. So for me that was very meaningful.

Student #4: For me, the first time I met [Adjuoa], she came in as a guest speaker in the very first course that I took from her over two and a half years ago, and in a brief thirty minute process it's like she gave so much of who she was to the group that at that point in time I knew that I would be taking classes from her before leaving this campus. It was just a done deal. She immediately got married and went off to Ghana and was out of here. So it's like I waited for almost a year and a half before getting to take a course from her . . . it was well worth the wait. It's exactly what [one student said] . . . for me it has to do with the safe space, which for me feels even more than safe. It's like I feel resourceful. I feel capable in her presence, and the class setting then becomes a place for me to stretch bigger than I've ever risked or stretched in my life. It's like all of the bounties just exist. And the other thing for me is that she's so grounded. Her actions are so grounded in what she believes that it's like that old thing . . . you walk your talk . . . she is phenomenal at that, and she does it at a conscious level as well as subconscious level.

Student #5: [Adjuoa] is my advisor, and I'll never forget the first day I saw her. I had come to the College of Education to find out what I needed to do to apply to the [doctoral] program, and I had just left a really great meeting with [a professor] and [I] was walking down the hallway, and this woman swung the door open from her office, and she was walking down the hallway, and she says, 'Good morning.' I thought I don't know who that is but that woman [is] going to be important in my life, and she has been a very important person to me. As a black woman preparing to be a part of the Academy, I can look to her and see that, sure, I can, [I] can be a part of the Academy in a real and authentic way. I don't have to bury and hide who I am. I don't have to wear a mask. I can take the mask off and be myself. That's really important to her, and you know that right away when you take a class from her because the first thing you do as a student in her class is to present yourself to the class in an autobiographical presentation of self. She is an incredible woman, and she is willing to risk stepping out there and living and sharing what she learns when she's going out there . . . always a teacher, always a researcher . . . that's [Adjuoa] . . . always teaching, always researching, always writing. It just blows my mind how she's always writing. She writes about everything, and it will be incredible to see what's in those journals that she writes one day when somebody discovers them and exposes us all.

Student #6: If I had to sum her up in one word it would be contagious. It's like you leave here, and she has taught me to be less critical and more accepting of differences, and I think that's one thing that really sticks out in my mind about her . . . that she's so open and so accepting that you do feel comfortable.

While listening to the students' testimonials, it reminded me of the way bell hooks (1994) describes teaching in her book Teaching to Transgress.

Based on the students' comments of Adjuoa's teaching practices, hooks (1994) would describe her teaching as engaged pedagogy constructing a practice of freedom. This practice combines an ethic of care and authenticity, as hooks (1994) offers:

> That learning process comes easiest to those of us who teach who also believe that there is an aspect of our vocation that is sacred; who believe that our work is not merely to share information but to share in the intellectual and spiritual growth of our students. To teach in a manner that respects and cares for the souls of our students is essential if we are to provide the necessary conditions where learning can most deeply and intimately begin.[3]

In a similar vein, Parker Palmer (1998) would describe Adjuoa's pedagogical practices by offering:

> Good teachers join self and subject and students in the fabric of life . . . Good teachers possess the capacity for connectedness. They are able to weave a complex web of connections among themselves, their subjects, and their students so that students can learn to weave a world for themselves . . . The connections made by good teachers are held not in their methods but in their hearts—meaning heart in its ancient sense, as the place where intellect and emotion and spirit and will converge in the human self. [4]

In this respect, Adjuoa shares her own words of wisdom, which has been significant in how she thinks of her work. She quoted one particular principle she lives by, which is biblical and written in Micah 6:8, "What does the Lord require of you, but to do justice, to love kindness, and to walk humbly with your God"[5] . . . that's what I'm required to do and that's what my work is all about.

THEME THREE: SPIRITUALLY GUIDED LEADERSHIP FOR SOCIAL JUSTICE

One of the most sacred relationships in organizations is that between people—those who lead and those who are being led. This relationship, which is a central part of working together, depends to an extraordinary degree on the clearly expressed and consistently demonstrated values of the leader as seen through the special lens of those who follow. Moreso, this relationship between individuals is why leadership and ethics are inextricably woven together.[6]

As noted by Collins (2000), "Black women intellectuals [including myself] who articulate an autonomous, self-defined standpoint are in a position to examine the usefulness of coalitions with other groups, both scholarly and activist, in order to develop new models for social change."[7] In many ways, this has been the case for the women in this study who have taken an inward spiritual journey, which has allowed them to do the continuous self-exploration, and the understandings that emerged have become critical in their respective leadership roles. As noted by Napier (1999), in School Leadership " . . . one must understand one's moral reasoning for wanting to perform leadership acts . . . [and] a desire to serve must be understood before a true commitment to making a difference can occur."[8] For Chaka, Adjuoa, and Jewel, it is evident in their narratives that their leadership and concern for others has been more important than their titles as deans. Once again, we cannot ignore nor erase the historical context of the lives of African-American women in this country knowingly and oftentimes unknowingly addressing interlocking systems of domination based on issues of race, class and gender. Bearing this in mind, these particular women, like their foremothers, have continuously been instrumental in addressing issues of social justice throughout their lives.

With respect to Chaka's, Adjuoa's, and Jewel's way of knowing and being as it relates to social justice in the academy, there were similar themes which emerged, such as: integrity, standing by principles, and risk taking.

Adjuoa's early educational experiences, consequently, have played a critical role in how she currently constructs her leadership and teaching. This became evident when she shared with me the following:

> . . . there were moments in school that I knew were not fair, that I knew were based on a judgment of me that was not true. I can say that now. I couldn't say that then. It just tore me up as a child, but I didn't know that then . . . now, the work of being a teacher, the work of being a professor becomes that of trying to right that wrong, if you will. Of trying to work against those sorts of experience of others like me and others in general. So, yes, there's no question that I've learned to be a teacher through lessons of my life, and it starts with my parents but works through schooling and some of the important experiences in schooling that have shaped me; not just powerfully and positive ones, but those I find myself working against now. But, I'm grateful for them because I'm not sure I would work as hard if I had not had [those experiences].

In turn, Adjuoa's leadership is demonstrated by the way she addresses various issues in her day-to-day practices through the embodiment of her spiritual self and maintaining congruency in her way of knowing and being whenever she has to take a stand. For instance, Adjuoa talked about how she deals with situations regarding racist or sexist practices by stating:

While I recognize racism and sexism, and work constantly to try to create spaces that are much more gentle and caring, and kind and loving, I don't spend a lot of time thinking about or battling against racism or sexism. People have their own opinions. They're going to say what they're going to say whether I engage them or not. The best I can do in those situations is to let folks know where they're wrong, but to do it in such a way . . . a friend of mine says I use my position and my work to cut to heal not to bleed and that's really what I attempt to do. I will be the first to call somebody out on a racist or sexist joke. I cut to heal, not to bleed or to harm. So I'm going to tell you about yourself, but it's not because I get a big thrill of telling you about yourself. It is not an ego invested in me telling you about yourself or calling you out, but I do want to let you know what you've just done because you may not be aware of that, and if you are I just want to let you know, again, that it isn't acceptable.

On the other hand, Jewel talked about her leadership and how she makes meaning of the various challenges she may be faced with by stating:

The first question that I always ask myself if things don't go my way is basically what you're asking is whether this is something that really needs to happen. How important is it that it go my way? How important is it that it go at all? And if my conclusion to that inquiry is that it's something beyond me . . . it's not just something that I want to do, but it's something that reasonably should happen and could happen, then my challenge is to find a way to make it happen. And I firmly believe that if it's good enough then I will find a way, and I've been pretty successful in that. There have been some things that I've said [that are] not worth it because [they are] not important enough. This is just not something that I was interested in, but if nobody is interested in it but me, then maybe it shouldn't happen. So, I guess that's if you're talking about leadership style, that's probably my leadership style. That when you lead, you lead the group, the collective, just kind of go out there and make your own world. So, if people don't want to come along with you, then that's a question of the kind of leadership that you're providing. If there's a negotiation to be done, how do you do that?

Jewel continued talking about the negotiation process:

The first thing I do is listen. I ask questions and I listen. And it may be once I listen I find out what there is to do or not do as it were. And I don't consider myself as the only one with brains, the only one with a past, the only one with a heart. You get people who are interested in doing the thing that you want to do. You try to work cooperatively with others to make that happen, and it has consistently worked for

> me. I believe, also, in a good communication network so you have to talk to people, you have to listen, you have to work, you've got to be persistent sometimes. You have to recognize change in small places. All those things.

In a similar way, Chaka discussed how she maintains her sense of integrity and stands by principles when dealing with challenging situations in her position as a dean. Chaka talked about several situations:

> There have been a couple of situations where there was an abuse of power on the part of a particular person, and I had to kind of call them on the carpet for that, and so I dealt with it very directly, and those are actually the easy ones. I would almost rather someone just blatantly violate something because then it's very clearcut. You call them on it. Procedure is so and so. You violated that. It's not appropriate. It will stop or whatever the consequences . . . pay the fine, lose your job, whatever. The most difficult ones for me are the ones where it's not like they're violating a rule or a procedure. It's not blatant where you can open up the code book and show them. But it's the principle of the thing, and I think that's where it gets a little hazy because I'm using a different guiding structure or framework or paradigm than they might be, so then it becomes almost a war of views and I can't say that I'm so right, so those for me are the most difficult. What I tend to do in those situations is sit down and really say look . . . here's how I'm looking at this situation . . . here is how your behavior is not helpful for you nor for the collective nor for whatever the situation is, and since I'm held responsible basically for the well being of this organization, here is how I am proposing we deal with this. Sometimes the person will acquiesce and say 'Okay,' sometimes they won't. And when they don't then I'm faced with, okay Chaka, you either say you will because I said so and the buck stops with me, or say, okay we'll do it your way, and then you go into it knowing that the by product of that is not going to be, at least in my view at the time, is not going to be healthy, and that's real difficult . . . What I tend to do then is, if I think the result will not just be totally detrimental to that person, they'll survive but they'll get some scraps, just say alright, and I'll let them get the scrapes.

Chaka shares another perspective on how she deals with ethical issues:

> I have had a situation where ethically it wasn't again a rule, but I knew this is just not the right thing to do, and so I will pull myself out of that situation and say, you know, I can't make you change this or I can't make you do this, but I feel it's wrong so I will not be party to it. So, I'm going on record as objecting, and then I just let it go and let them know why I don't think it's appropriate and why I'm removing myself.

THEME FOUR: LEADING BEYOND THE BORDERS OF ACADEME

For every African-American woman who makes it in the professional world, there is probably another badge of identification beyond her career status—that of being involved in her community or organizations beyond the borders of her work location. Whether consciously or unconsciously derived, these multiple locations of leadership provides space for one to become involved with a particular "cause or action," which proves invaluable to one's own soul satisfaction along with a continued need to carry the torch of the many women and men who have paved the path for African-Americans in this country. Hence, African-American women hold a long tradition of community activism and serving as change agents in whatever space or place of location they occupy. Brewer (1997) supports this idea by stating that African-American women "have always linked themselves to the broader black struggle."[9] While African-American women's activism remains just as prevalent today, there are two particular observations of the women in this study that must be noted: (1) this community activism extends beyond the Academy and the African-American community; and (2) this activism does not limit one from having an overall impact on the larger society regardless of race, class, creed, nationality or gender.

When tracing the stream of history of African Americans prior to the 1960's, one would find more segregated communities where teachers, doctors, lawyers, and working class people lived together. This was especially true for the lives of Anna Julia Cooper, Lucy Diggs Slowe, and Mary McLeod Bethune who were considered the "race women" of their time—they were activists both in their professions and their communities.

Like their foremothers, the women in this study will be considered the "race women" of their time for generations to come. Let us not forget the historical reflections and vast contributions African Americans have made in America, thus "the story of African-American people is a glorious one, replete with a pantheon of mighty voices and courageous souls who in their combined strength have overcome inestimable odds and carved a special niche in the gallery of world culture."[10]

Though Jewel does not have a long list of community activities that she is involved with at this time, she holds a history of being active in other communities that were predominantly African-American (previously mentioned in Chapter Four). Today, however, Jewel is far more inundated with her leadership role as a dean and her publishing within Academia. Though little attention was given to the role she plays conducting a teacher's workshop every year outside of the university, this endeavor can be seen as a form of activism. Jewel has even been honored for her leadership role in working with this project. When I asked Jewel whether or not she was involved with any activities outside of the university, she modestly responded that she was not active outside of her publishing community. Oddly enough, I learned by examining Jewel's university website that she had been honored with a teaching award by the state for this project.

On the other hand, Chaka's work extends beyond the university. She serves on the community school board where she resides, which is located in a different area where she works. Chaka has been involved with the school board for six years. Not only has she shown a vested interest in her work and community, she has also responded to the vocation of helping her students beyond the everyday practice of either teaching or mentoring. Chaka shared with me an occasion when she had a particular graduate student working with her who needed assistance with some very personal issues, and she took her home for the weekend to help her sort out these issues and get back on track with school.

In contrast, Adjuoa clearly defines community in a broader sense by stating that her work extends beyond the university and the borders of the United States. Adjuoa, as noted in her biographical sketch, has been named a chief in an African village in Ghana, West Africa, where she has built a school.

In the Ghanaian culture, an "outsider" can be named a chief when he/she has made a significant contribution to the development of the tribal community. Adjuoa talked about her situated identity and how she is comfortable in serving in these two very different roles in African and American culture. Here, she stated:

> . . . there's a possibility for how a sister who does this thing on one side can do this other thing totally different on the other. I mean in some ways people see my lives as two very different things. The example somebody gave me the other day is on one continent you're a queen and on the other continent you're a dean, and those lives seem very, very different for most people. They're very similar for me but they're very different, and because we know so little about the continent of Africa, particularly as African Americans, the thought that I could be doing my wash by hand doesn't fit with the idea of being an Associate Dean. The thought that I would live in a place that doesn't have air conditioning, that I don't have a car, I don't have access to a computer, I don't have a phone. Those things don't live with the Associate Dean role. That [I'm in Ghana] digging in the dirt and building bricks versus living in my office . . . . So folks are very enamored with the possibility of how you do that life in two different places in such very radical ways.
>
> For me they're incredibly congruent lives, but for those who have never had that experience . . . so Portia [an African-American woman] would say, 'Girl, I don't know what you're doing there on the conti-

> nent, but when you get it all done and you get [things] in place and you get me a fan, I might come see you, but keep doing this stuff on this side, in case we can persuade you to go into the Deanship, we want to be able to do that.'

After examining the various themes, which emerged from these three women's stories, it is evident that through their language and the way they talk about their lives—a spiritual dimension very much embodies their way of knowing and being. As Fairholm (1997) notes, "It is the spiritual knowledge that is essential . . . . It is what we are, who we are, and why we think we are here in life that ultimately guides our individual lives and conditions our relationships with others."[11] In this same respect, the lives of Adjuoa, Chaka and Jewel will be further examined in Chapter Six, which will help to fully explicate how they make meaning of their lives through their own stories and the various theories which help to inform their leadership practices.

CHAPTER 6

Still Lifting as We Climb

I leave you finally a responsibility to our young people . . . . Our children must never lose their zeal for building a better world. They must not be discouraged from aspiring greatness, for they are to be the leaders of tomorrow. —Mary McLeod Bethune

COLLINS' (2000) CONCEPTUAL FRAMEWORK OF BLACK FEMINIST THOUGHT broadly defines African-American women's feminist/womanist positioning and how we experience the world in multiple dimensions. African-American women's identity politics are as varied as women from any other culture. Our feminisms and ways of knowing exemplify that we are by no means monolithic. Yet, there are some cultural forms, which permeate throughout African-American culture identifiable to us, such as the spiritual nature of our lives, how we talk about our lives and make meaning of our experiences. As noted by Collins (2000), a Black woman's standpoint can be viewed as culturally specific, but it does not attempt to essentialize the African-American woman. Hence, " . . . culture itself is dynamic and changing, the enduring themes characterizing a Black women's standpoint become shaped in dialogue with actual social practices."[1] At the same time it can be said that the cultural landscape of African-American women's spirituality and experiences in this country shares some common ground.

Khaula Murtadha-Watts (1999) suggests these same notions in her work on African-American women in leadership, saying that our positions often draw upon profound historical traditions of inner spiritual strength as well as an activist ethic of risk/urgency. In terms of culture and language, African-American women symbolically use forms of God-talk, moving and acting in conversations with "God," "asking of the Good Lord," "the

Spirit," "Providence," and the many ways of spirituality in their lives. In turn, African-American women are strengthened to set goals, to see hope and possibility, and to love in spite of the various gains and losses they have encountered.[2]

The nature of African-American women's standpoint offers a cultural context embedded within their spiritual leadership, which is further analyzed by the various themes in this section. Along with Stewart's cultural context of spirituality outlined in Chapter Two, I reiterate how I am attempting to make sense of African-American women's lives and the way they make meaning of their spirituality. I am interested in developing an understanding of the women's sense of self, sense of mission and purpose in life, and how they make personal meaning of their work, as well as knowing there is a belief in a higher power greater than one's self.

In consideration of the various theories supporting this research, I reexamine the various themes outlined in Chapter Five through the trajectory of spirituality, feminism/womanism, and leadership. As I address each theme in this chapter, I introduce one or more theories, which support each theme most appropriately. For example, feminist/womanist theory may be used in addressing one particular theme versus another. For the sake of avoiding redundancy, I may refer to one particular participant in each theme without repeating all three women's voices; yet their experiences have been quite similar. The reader should continue to bear in mind that the various theories inform who these women are, as well as shed light on their leadership practices. By integrating these theories at this point, it again helps one to understand how these women make meaning of their spirituality and leadership on a day-to-day basis.

THEME ONE: SPIRITUALLY GUIDED LEADERSHIP THROUGH SERVANTHOOD

For the three women in this study, the phenomenon of servanthood resonates when discussing their leadership and work within Academia and beyond. The notion of servanthood becomes even clearer when Adjuoa, Chaka, and Jewel define their work by using words such as "servant," "service," "serving others," and/or "working for a higher purpose or calling." Furthermore, this service is far greater than being recognized for the titles they hold (previously noted in Chapter Five). Clearly, the title or role of these women does not define who they are, and their role is not as important as the work they do. L. A. Napier (1999) affirms this by stating that leaders must not become their role. Yet, leaders must know and keep in mind who they are, however, "a defined purpose of what really matters" will keep one's soul alive."[3] The manner in which the women in this study talk about serving others demonstrates what is important to them and indicates that their leadership is not based on self-interest, but rather that the interests of others is placed at the forefront. Robert Heifetz (1998) notes that many leaders start out with a clear purpose but somewhere along the way lose sight of the significance of that purpose.[4] Here, I would like to suggest that this is not the case for Adjuoa, Chaka, and Jewel because the spiritual nature of their lives keeps them grounded and reminds them of their purpose in everything they do in life, which is for a "higher spiritual calling" than what one might visibly recognize in an organization.

At this point, I revisit the way Chaka talks about her leadership, which is very similar to the other two women in this study. For example, Chaka referred to her leadership as being a servant to others. As she stated, "I think the ultimate leader is the person who can serve the people. Now that service means facilitating the needs of the people being met, organization, whatever it is you're leading."

Fairholm (1997) offers his view advancing the discourse of spiritual leadership and servanthood in his book *Capturing the Heart of Leadership:*

> Spiritual leadership asks us to reject past models of human leadership, which focused on values of self-interest. The energy driving these earlier models were implicit values focusing on power, wealth, and prestige. Power, wealth and prestige are not definitive of spiritual leaders. Rather, the transcendent values of spiritual leaders include a rejection of self-interest and a focus on servanthood.[5]

Just as Adjuoa, Chaka and Jewel, have described their leadership by terms such as "servant," and "serving others, " language such as "facilitator," and "enabler" can also be added to this list as they described their leadership. Fairholm (1997) affirms this spiritually guided leadership by stating:

> Stewardship and service are intimately related. Servant and steward may be more similar roles than they appear on first thought. *Servant*, in ancient Greek, means one who is dedicated to service on behalf of another. The Greek root of *steward* means a household servant, one who superintends a household. Stewardship means being accountable without control or forced compliance.[6]

Fairholm (1997) continues:

> The steward-leader is servant first. The leader's sense of stewardship operates on two levels. The first is stewardship for the people they lead. The second is a stewardship for the larger purpose of mission that underlies the larger enterprise. The steward-leader demonstrates these type of skills: building shared vision, surfacing and challenging mental models, and systems thinking.7

Clearly, both the ends and means are critical to stewardship, and as Fairholm notes, "How we do work is as important as what we do."[8] In many ways, how Adjuoa, Chaka, and Jewel talked about how they do their work by placing the people they serve at the center versus themselves parallels closely with Fairholm's description of servanthood and stewardship. In advancing this notion of serving others, leadership theorist James MacGregor Burns (1994) describes this type of leadership as transformational leadership. Burns posits that people begin with the need for survival and security, and once those needs are met, concern themselves with "higher" needs like affection, belonging, the common good, and serving others.[9]

THEME TWO: A CALL TO CONSCIOUSNESS IN EVERYDAY PRACTICE: EXERCISING AN ETHIC OF CARE

By developing and maintaining an ethic of care, African-American women have carried forth a sense of consciousness that has been handed down through past generations by other African-American women and men who have paved the way. Traditionally, the African-American community has imparted to each generation to be active in building their community and "giving back" to others who may be less fortunate. Whether "giving back" occurs within the academic community or the communities where Adjuoa, Chaka, and Jewel reside, it is evident that this work is being carried out. Hence, it is the incremental changes that occur on a day-to-day basis that in turn transforms our larger society.

As noted by Collins (2000) there are three inter-related components of the ethic of caring which include: (1) the value placed on individual uniqueness/expressiveness, (2) the appropriateness of emotions, and (3) the capacity for empathy.[10] When talking about individual expressiveness, Collins (2000) stands in agreement with Paris (1995) and Ani (1997), by stating, "Rooted in a tradition of African humanism, each individual is thought to be a unique expression of a common spirit, power, or energy inherent in all life."[11] The second component concerning the appropriateness of emotions refers to the way emotions are imbued through dialogue; hence, emotion indicates that a speaker believes in the validity of their knowledge claim. The final component involves developing the capacity for empathy, which has allowed African-American women to develop an understanding of others' positions in life whether it's been through examining literature, one's own standpoint or lived experience, or listening and learning from other individuals' stories.

In listening to the women in this study, it is evident that a caring relationship takes place with faculty, students and other administrators who they encounter on a day-to-day basis. None of these women take the notion of mentoring lightly, though they are called upon to be mentors to a number of African-American students and students of color by the mere fact that the majority of people (operating from a Eurocentric paradigm) identify them as being a part of an oppressed group, thus having some experience with knowing how others may feel or better understanding other individuals' marginalized positions. On the one hand, this could very well be the case; however, on the other hand this is a very essentialist notion oftentimes played out in a majority setting. Despite the essentialist possibility, these three African-American women have taken it upon themselves to serve as mentors, "othermothers," and change agents creating and opening spaces for others in the Academy.

As previously noted in Adjuoa's narrative in Chapter Five, her students talked about her leadership in various ways such as being a mentor, "othermother," and change agent. One particular student specifically described her as serving as both a mentor, and mother to him. In his words (Student #1):

> She's that thought that makes you smile . . . like a son doing good for his mother . . . she creates a space where I want to be so good at everything that I do in her class for her . . . I know that by being the best that I can be as a student . . . I am becoming better as a person, as a student, as an educator, as an African-American male . . . she really makes me want to challenge who I am and challenge what I am good at as a student and as a professional.

In *Deep Change*, Robert Quinn (1996) offers a view of personal leadership, which helps to describe Adjuoa in a way that very much resonates with this student's voice (and the other students in Chapter Five) along with the way Adjuoa talks about her life and leadership. Quinn (1996) states:

> One key to successful leadership is continuous personal change. Personal change is a reflection of our inner growth and empowerment. Empowered leaders are the only ones who can induce real change. They can forcefully communicate at a level beyond telling. By having the courage to change themselves, they model the behavior they are asking of others. Clearly understood by almost everyone, this message, based in integrity, is incredibly powerful. It builds trust and credibility and helps others confront the risk of empowering themselves.[12]

In this regard, Quinn's (1996) description of leadership ties closely with the way Adjuoa views her leadership, and one particular principle which serves as a guide comes from Micah 6:8: "'What does the Lord require of you, but to do justice, to love kindness, and to walk humbly with your God'[13] . . . that's what I'm required to do and that's what my work is all about."

In a similar vein, I can attest to the relationship I have developed with Chaka as a mentor, and the way I have observed her working with others. While working with Chaka, I have had the opportunity not only to seek guidance on my assigned duties in program development, but also to seek advice on my own academic and career endeavors. Our "kindred spirits" allowed us to develop a relationship of mentoring and friendship to the extent that I would feel comfortable seeking advice regardless of whether the issues were academic, professional or personal. This mentoring relationship also extended to the classroom. I approached Chaka one semester and asked her if she would be willing to teach a class with me if it were approved, and she agreed. This teaching experience extended beyond teaching one course to two different courses. During one semester, we taught the course *Black Psychology*, and during another semester, we taught *U.S. Feminisms and the Diaspora*. Teaching both of these classes with Chaka proved to be one of the best teaching experiences I have had in my doctoral program. When I spoke of "kindred spirits" earlier, this encounter became more real by the way students would ask us to respond to various questions, and often, we both would offer either the same or very similar views. One day during our seminar on *Black Psychology*, students asked us to respond to a particular question, and we both answered with similar responses. What became surprising to the students were our hand gestures, facial expressions and the way we crossed our legs as a part of the reaction. This behavior did not become evident to us until after class, when several students came to share with us in laughter what had occurred in class while we were sitting before them. I share this particular experience to provide the reader with a brief history of the type of relationship I have shared with Chaka.

On the other hand, I have observed several undergraduate and graduate students seeking Chaka's mentoring and "mothering." I have observed students stop by Chaka's office just to say "hello" and give her an update on how things were going with their courses. One afternoon while meeting with Chaka, a student from one of our classes dropped by the office to share his poetry with us. We stopped in the middle of our meeting, and joined him in the courtyard outside of the building (as he had requested), which set the stage for his poetry reading on this sunny and warm spring day. Embedded within this student's poetry were strong social and political messages regarding issues of race and gender. When the student completed the reading, we talked with him for a while about what inspired him to write this particular piece of poetry.

In examining the phenomenon of "othermothering" by African-American women in their life and leadership, Collins (2000), and James and Busia (1994), elucidate its significance and the ways in which it is demonstrated. The experiences of African-American women as othermothers in their work and communities provide a foundation for conceptualizing Black women's political activism. As associated with one's personal experience, Collins (2000) offers that experiences such as being both nurtured as children and being held responsible for siblings and fictive kin within the kin networks stimulated a generalized ethic of care and personal accountability for African-American women.[14] These women not only felt that they should be accountable to their own kin, but should also create a bond with all of the children within the Black community. Within this ethic of care, as African-American women became more highly educated, it was expected of them to use their education in a socially responsible way.

As Collins (2000) notes, the community othermother tradition also explains the 'mothering the mind' relationships that can develop between African-American women teachers and their Black female and male students.[15] " . . . The community othermother role—namely, Black women's support for education—illustrates the important dimension of Black women's political activism. Education has long served as a powerful symbol for the important connections among self, change, and empowerment in African-American communities.[16] Interestingly, James and Busia (1994) discuss the status of the community othermother as being "bestowed upon women who are often over 40 years of age, not only because over time they have exhibited an ethic of care so critical to the survival and well-being of their communities, but also because they have lived long enough to have a sense of the community's tradition and culture."[17] In fully explicating what it means to be an "othermother," James and Busia (1994) provide characteristics of the "othermother" by offering:

> The woman's behavior as a mother and/or othermother has been exemplary and she is considered to be wise. Commanding a powerful position of respect as a result of these characteristics, the community othermother was/is able successfully to critique the behavior of individual members of the community and to provide them with directions on appropriate behavior(s). Based upon her knowledge and her respected position, a community othermother is also in a position to provide analyses and/or critiques of conditions or situations that may affect the well being of her community.[18]

It is clear that the phenomenon of "othermothering" derives from an African/African-American ethos, and the way in which the three women in this study describe the way they relate to their students in many ways exemplifies this "othermothering" taking place. Yet, I would like to go a step further and suggest that for the women in this study, the phenomenon of "othermothering" can exist with students from any ethnic background, especially since they are located at majority institutions and the majority of their students are not African-American. Culturally speaking, and from my own experience, I would like to suggest that more than likely African-American students would be more inclined to identify and seek out these othermothers on their campus.

This ethic of care not only has to do with these women's sense of mentoring, and "othermothering," but it also has to do with a sense of consciousness by creating and opening spaces for others who have been traditionally marginalized. The unique position of African-American women confronting oppressive forces embedded within the trajectory of race, class, and gender offers the women in this study a different lens from which they possibly have observed, witnessed and attested to their own experience being identified as a marginalized group. Marginality does not necessarily have to be seen as a place of deprivation; it can be seen as a place for radical possibility, a space of resistance.[19] "Understanding marginality as [a] position and place of resistance is crucial for oppressed, exploited, [and] colonized people...these margins have been both sites of repression and sites of resistance" notes bell hooks.[20] Hence, the experiences of the three women in this study places them in a position to hold a level of sensitivity and understanding toward others who may have suffered or have been placed in a position of marginality.

While working with Chaka as a Teaching/Research Associate, I initially learned of her various roles and responsibilities as an Associate Dean. Chaka's work primarily deals with faculty development and issues concerning members of the faculty. In addition, Chaka has several responsibilities concerning issues of diversity. For example, she serves as a representative/liaison for the graduate students of color at her university, she assists in the organization of diversity and educational programs for high school students, and she also serves as the initiator for the "Diversity Enrichment" program for the faculty. In a similar way, both Jewel and Adjuoa talked about their role and responsibility in working with faculty and students.

By the way Adjuoa, Chaka, and Jewel talked about their leadership, they conveyed in their language how they view themselves and the way they relate to others. In their narratives they speak of possibilities to change the world in a very different way than the traditional leadership paradigm. For example, Adjuoa refers to her leadership as being led by something beyond her role and having a purpose for the work she does. In essence, Adjuoa's being led for a greater purpose has to do with, " . . . opening up opportunities for people to be their best selves . . . It's about creating spaces of peace in the world and walking in love."

In a different way, Jewel describes her leadership in very modest terms by saying that she doesn't necessarily consider herself to be a leader [in the traditional sense] but she thinks of herself as being a "facilitator of things and as an enabler." Jewel also commented, "I'm not one who particularly likes being out front controlling other people. I rather see things emerge.

I'd rather see growth. . . ." Jewel's downplaying of her position of authority as a leader is in line with Heifetz (1998), who states that people who lead without authority lead across two boundaries. These two boundaries include: the boundary of their formal organization, and the boundary defined by the wider network of people with whom they have gained informal authority (trust, respect, and moral persuasion).[21]

Adjuoa, Chaka and Jewel convey a consciousness embodying a deep sense of care along with a moral and ethical responsibility, which is very much embedded in the ethos of their leadership. In support of the these women's leadership practices, Parker Palmer (1992), offers Vaclav Havel's words of wisdom in his work on spirituality, by stating, "Consciousness precedes being...and the salvation of the world lies within the human heart."[22] In his own words, Palmer (1992) describes the function of the human heart in leading and changing society by stating, "Spirit is. Consciousness is. Human awareness is. Thought is. Spirituality is."[23] These are the deep sources of freedom and power, which have allowed people to move boulders and create change.[24] Like Palmer (1992), I posit that the insight of our spiritual world is not to deny the reality of the outer world. Rather, it helps us to understand that we create that world, in part, by projecting our spirit on it—for better or worse.

THEME THREE: SPIRITUALLY GUIDED LEADERSHIP FOR SOCIAL JUSTICE

When we discuss issues of inequality regarding race, class, gender and other forms of oppression that may occur knowingly or unknowingly, we are addressing the discourse of social inequalities for social justice. For some individuals, it has become elusive as to what social justice means in our society because of one's privilege or situated identity which allows them to maintain an oblivious state of being; thus, social justice implies coexisting with other individuals who must grapple with these issues on a day-to-day basis in order to help create a better world for everyone. Clearly, one person's privileged position can in turn become another person's oppressive way of life. On virtually any given day, we can read about issues of racism, sexism, classism, homophobic tensions, and so on, taking place throughout our country. The school violence that has taken place over the last couple of years with young girls being killed in Jonesboro (1998); students of different ethnic backgrounds, sexual orientations, and group affiliations shot down in Colorado (1999); and other violent rampages in California (2001) and Pennsylvania (2001) serve as real cases in point. At the same time, we can examine similar incidents that have also taken place on college campuses throughout this country. Yet, we do not have to look farther than in our own backyard—for me, Miami

University—which has reported various issues regarding racism, sexual harassment, assaults on gay individuals, and so on. As a society, we have become spiritually bankrupt to the extent of lacking a moral and/or ethical consciousness to the point of maintaining a blind eye to the perpetuation of these social ills. Then the question remains, how do we change such oppressive forms of marginalization when our institutions very much mirror our society?

In another vein, Larson and Murtadha (2001) discuss ideas of social justice regarding schools in our country by stating:

> . . . if inequity has been institutionalized in the theories, norms and practices of our society, and if researchers and administrators reify inequity and injustice by failing to examine, question and redress the inequities they see, then there is much to be done. Researchers in educational administration who believe that injustice in our schools and communities is neither natural nor inevitable loosely coalesce under an umbrella of inquiry called leadership for social justice.[25]

Though the women in this study do not attempt to hold all of the answers to how we should address these various issues, their own standpoint offers quite a different lens on how to view the world and make meaning of the world. Yet, their leadership practices offer ways in which we can begin to examine and consider the use of these practices on a much broader scale.

Similar to Adjuoa and Jewel, Chaka's words resonate as she talks about her life and how she makes meaning of her leadership. Chaka describes herself as being a "servant," and she commented, "the ultimate leader is the person who can serve the people."

Recognizing that language is a critical signifier in one's cultural frame of reference, it is especially important by the way these three women talk about themselves and their leadership in the meaning-making process. Again, the language imbued by the African-American women in this study evokes an ethos of the "nommo" (See Chapter One). In support of one's meaning making, Ngugi Wa Thiong'O (1986) shares insights on the notion of language by stating, "the choice of language and the use to which it is put is central to a people's definition of themselves in relation to their natural and social environment, indeed in relation to the entire universe."[26]

In examining the way these African-American women make meaning of their spirituality and leadership within the Ivory Tower and operating in spaces of contested terrain, Henry Giroux's (1993) *Border Crossings* offers the following:

> . . . it is the domain of language that the traces of a theoretical and political journey begin to emerge as part of a broader attempt to engage meaning as a form of social memory, social institutions as pow-

> erful carriers and legitimators of meaning, and social practices as sites in which meaning is re-invented in the body, desire, and in the relations between self and others.[27]

Having said this, it is clear that African-American women's ways of knowing and seeing the world embody a different form of leadership, disrupting the traditional male-centered hierarchal notions that have embodied organizations for the last century. Hence, it is language in all of its complexity which becomes central not only in the production of meaning and social identities but also as a constitutive condition for human agency.[28] The way these African-American women speak of their lives, the language inscribed by them which gives form to those modes of address, constitute their sense of the political, ethical, economic, and social way of being.

In varying degrees, Adjuoa, Chaka, and Jewel discussed the discursive practices in addressing issues of social justice and how they maintain their sense of integrity while taking an unwavering stand about any number of issues. For example, Adjuoa makes it plain by the way she deals with issues of racist or sexist practices as she states:

> While I recognize racism and sexism and work constantly to try to create spaces that are much more gentle and caring, and kind and loving, I don't spend a lot of time thinking about or battling against racism or sexism. People have their own opinions. They're going to say what they're going to say whether I engage them or not. The best I can do in those situations is to let folks know where they're wrong, but to do it in such a way . . . a friend of mine says I use my position and my work to cut to heal not to bleed, and that's really what I attempt to do. I will be the first to call somebody out on a racist or sexist joke. I cut to heal, not to bleed or to harm. So I'm going to tell you about yourself. It is not an ego invested in me telling you about yourself or calling you out, but I do want to let you know what you've just done because you may not be aware of that, and if you are I just want to let you know that it isn't acceptable.

In similar ways, Jewel and Chaka talked about ways in which they address various situations while maintaining a sense of integrity and standing by principles in the midst of dealing with various challenges. The process of inspiring others to change certain behaviors for the benefit of all has to be done in a way that connects to those whom the leader is attempting to inspire. In essence, to inspire someone means that the leader must appeal on a different level than mere motive . . . and therefore, must connect at the level of the spirit. As Fairholm (1999) states, someone inspires when they take us outside our routine ways of thinking and behaving and leads us to another higher level of interaction and focus.[29] Hence, spiritual leaders inspire followers and provide a helpful setting for this interactive relationship to take place. Spiritual leaders set the example by the way "they walk their walk, and talk their talk." Spiritual leaders provide the climate and conditions within which the leader's personal needs and the particular personal needs of the follower group can be juxtaposed in ways that let the one inspire the other.[30]

THEME FOUR: LEADING BEYOND THE BORDERS OF ACADEME

Throughout the history of African-American women's lives in American culture, they have had to take on multiple roles whether it was by choice or by circumstance. These roles were as multi-faceted as the women themselves. Whether the women served in the community, the church, the school, or within various organizations, they were usually involved in one or more arenas simultaneously along with holding a full-time job. The multiplicity of roles and responsibilities is evident in Chapter One in examining the lives of the foremothers. It is just as true today for the women in this study of their involvement beyond the academic arena at their designated university. Interestingly, the way Adjuoa, Chaka, and Jewel discuss their activism and involvement beyond their role as a dean is as varied as each person. Because we are not monolithic, it can be expected that the various ways in which these women are actively involved would differ. On the other hand, what differs today versus forty or fifty years ago is the fact that the composition of two of these women's communities has changed drastically. Therefore, the way they talk about community and the way they are involved in community differs drastically from their foremothers lives over eighty years ago, and it also differs from their own mother's lives over forty years ago. Admittedly, I was somewhat surprised and found it quite perplexing to hear how these three women talked about community and how they have resituated the meaning of community.

First, Adjuoa, unlike the other two women in this study, did not grow up in a predominantly African-American community. If the reader recalls, Adjuoa grew up in a very multicultural community in the Northwest part of the country. She has resituated the meaning of community to extend to the work she is doing in Ghana, West Africa. Quite clearly, community has more to do with how Adjuoa walks with the world and how she becomes involved in the places where she locates herself. As noted earlier in this study, Adjuoa is building a school in Ghana. In this West African community, Adjuoa has also been named a chief of the village where the school is being built.

Though Chaka grew up in a predominantly African-American community in the Midwest, she can no longer look out her door and say the people around her neighborhood are predominantly African-American.

Therefore, Chaka stays involved in community activities with her family through the Black church she attends. Chaka and her children are also invited to attend "Jack and Jill," a predominantly African-American 'high' society organization which fosters growth and development for the children of the families involved. Chaka is also active with the school board in her school district where she is often called upon to consult with school officials on various educational issues. By training, Chaka is an educational psychologist whose expertise is often sought after by school officials.

Similar to Chaka, Jewel grew up in a predominantly African-American community, and she was taught to be of service to her community. However, Jewel no longer lives in a predominantly African-American community, and how she talks about her activism is quite different. Jewel modestly discussed with me how she places most of her emphasis on publishing, and that particular group has become her community where she does her activist work. Interestingly enough, Jewel did not mention her work with teachers for a summer program until after I brought it up in the conversation. I learned of this information when I was viewing her university's web site and learned that she had been awarded for her outstanding work with this summer program.

From an historical perspective, and in the traditional sense of using the word "activism," African-American women's work has been broadly defined mostly from a grassroots level confronting everyday practices of sexism, classism, racism, or various other "isms" and issues that need to be addressed within the African-American community. Today, however, African-American women's activism extends beyond the grassroots to the international level, and continues to be defined and addressed in multiple ways. For the most part, this is evident in the lives of Adjuoa, Chaka, and Jewel as they have broadly defined their activism. Kimberly Springer (1999) supports this type of activism by offering a myriad of ways in which activism takes place today for African-American women. For instance, activism may take place in the form of "direct action" or activism involving face-to-face interaction with members of the community.[31] On the other hand, activism that might be considered intellectual and, hence, removed from street-level direct action which could include the following: writing as resistance, political education, consciousness raising, autobiography as "political witnessing," public statements in major U.S. newspapers, and filing lawsuits.[32] By discussing how the women in this study redefine their activism, there is no intent to situate this activism in a hierarchical form, hence suggesting that one form of activism is better than another. Conversely, the intent is to show how these women's activism is taking place beyond the Academy and to offer that these different forms of activism further the overall cause of social justice. As noted by Springer (1999), "African-American women's acts of 'everyday resistance' and intellectual work coexist to create positive, lasting change in the lives of African Americans"[33] and many others regardless of race, class, gender or sexual orientation.

In *Black Women in the Academy*, Josie R. Johnson (1997) discusses the lives of senior-level African-American women administrators; she states that these women must be able to understand the culture of higher education and be able to communicate within this culture in order to excel. Thus, African-American women must also be multicultural, and they have to know not only their own community but also the other communities so that they know how to represent and communicate the needs of the diverse communities.[34]

On the other hand, in examining the activism of Adjuoa, Chaka, and Jewel, and the way in which their spirituality manifests itself in their everyday leadership and activism, Stewart (1999) offers:

> Since blacks have not historically been able to integrate themselves fully into white America's community of the self as fully integrated beings, spirituality has allowed them to create significant patterns of personal existence that would instead create a community of self that would promote self unity and collective unity among African Americans.[35]

By the way these women talk about their lives and make meaning of their spirituality and leadership on a day-to-day basis, it becomes even clearer that the work they do is very much connected to who they are and their values in promoting positive change in their defined communities. Like Stewart (1999), I would like to suggest that, for these women, their spirituality has served as a humanizing function in creating self-unity by providing a higher sense of purpose and value in a world that has intentionally sought to demean and destroy them.[36] Hence, African-American spirituality remains one of the humanizing, radicalizing, and holistic forces in the Black experience. In turn, African Americans have "practiced a freedom of expression that directly defies the various processes of devaluation and repression of the larger society . . . this freedom is integral to self-sanity and collective unity."[37] African Americans, nevertheless, must speak their minds through the soul force that establishes the self as a viable entity in society, which is a part of being Black in America. Yet, it is this "freedom to interpret, value, express, and construct an existence that reinforces positive norms for self and community."[38]

SUMMARY

I have examined the lives of the three women in this study, and how they have made meaning of their spirituality and leadership in various ways, and I do not suggest that these stories resonate in the lives of all African-American women in higher education administration. Yet, I do believe that there are many African-American women who can relate to these stories in the way in which they lead their own lives. For me, it is important to let the lives of Adjuoa, Chaka, and Jewel speak without attempting to speak for them. Feminist standpoint epistemologies challenge how truth is known and identify subjective experience as a critical source of social knowledge; it is just as critical in understanding the way these women have talked about their lives. As noted by Aaronette M. White (1999), "rather than seeking a single truth about a phenomenon, research guided by recent feminist standpoint epistemologies seeks to uncover the multifaceted nature of women's reality or 'multiple truths' that are shaped by different sociopolitical contexts."[39]

In *The Drama of Leadership*, Starratt (1993) metaphorically discusses the various ways in which people with organizations carry out their day-to-day responsibilities through dramatic acts of working within the organization. Based upon my own experience working in higher education and serving as a doctoral student, there is no question in my mind that the organizational culture and the organizational politics that take place on a day-to-day basis are very much embedded within the drama. Essentially, it is the drama being staged and acted out throughout various points depending upon the day, week, and the type of activities taking place on the college campus. Dramatic acts located in different spaces at the university can all impinge upon each other at any given moment. It is important to take note of this drama because of the way Adjuoa, Chaka, and Jewel have talked about their lives. Inasmuch as their positions place them within the dramatic framework, it is quite intriguing to hear the language they use to develop a sense of understanding of how they make meaning of their own lives and leadership. Spirituality remains at the core of their leadership, and has served as a way for these women to deal with the drama in a peaceful and harmonious manner. It is spirituality that allows them to handle adverse situations without framing them as such. It is spirituality which allows them to deal with difficult people and situations, to recognize the drama occurring as it does, but still does not allow it to shatter their sense of being. It is spirituality that allows them to stay focused on the important issues and keep the student in mind as they do their job. It is spirituality which reminds them everyday of why they are in the Academy having an impact on faculty, students, and administrators. It is spirituality that serves as the empowering resistance, and allows these women to maintain their sense of moral and ethical character without compromising or sacrificing their principles for someone else. The empowering resistance becomes evident when these women can identify situations, which may not be morally or ethically sound, and then take a stand on them, or they may have no other choice than to walk away from the situation knowing they have provided their best guidance and assistance in the situation. It is these women's spirituality that manifests itself in the "nommo" through the "God-talk" Khaula Murtahda-Watts (2001) refers to regarding the way women speak of themselves. It is the "God-talk" that encourages these women to excel, to be confident, and to know that they are making a difference in the world around them whether serving at the university or within other communities. It is their spirituality and God-talk combined that keeps these women centered and grounded in maintaining their lives as servants and providing service to others. It is the spiritual nature of these women's lives whose stories became real to me as I have been working on this study. It is these women's voices, that spoke to me from the pages of the transcripts, and inspired me to believe, "Rochelle, you can do this, and don't let anyone turn you around"—both the contemporary women and the foremothers in this study.

CHAPTER 7

Our Spiritual Strivings

IN THIS STUDY I HAVE SHARED A PORTION OF THE LIVES OF THREE AFRICAN-American women deans and showed how their leadership is guided by something much larger than themselves . . . their spirituality. As I have noted throughout this work, the purpose of this study has been to examine the ways in which African-American women make meaning of their spiritual selves in their everyday leadership practices. Subsequently, I have noted another consideration as a part of the landscape of these women's lives, namely how they have negotiated spaces of difference through their spiritual leadership, and how it has had an impact on the social, cultural, and political construct of a male-dominated arena. In this final chapter, I first discuss particular findings and dispel any myths or assumptions of my own coming into this study. Second, I address particular ways in which the spiritual leadership of African-American women in the Academy could have possibly played a role in the new cultural politics taking place within the Ivory Tower.

While I found that certain assumptions were confirmed, I uncovered a number of other "happenings" which caused me to take a pause and reposition the lens in a way I thought might be appropriate for these three African-American women. First, one finding is the way these women have resituated community. In particular, what I thought they might express about the communities where they resided was not necessarily the case. For example, these women live in predominantly White communities and do not necessarily engage with their neighbors to any large extent. Whereas, thirty to forty years ago, it was not uncommon for most African Americans to grow up in predominantly Black communities, which meant that everyone knew their neighbors and more than likely had some type of interaction with them. Second, based on the age range of these women, between forty and fifty years old, the assumption was that they more than likely grew up in predominantly Black communities and attended predominantly Black schools during their formative years, which was not the case either. Third, because of their upward mobility, and the fact that they no longer live in predominantly Black communities, they no longer participate directly in community activities. In many ways, these women have redefined community, and their participation or activism extends far beyond the immediate community in which they reside. This particular phenomenon was confirmed by the experiences of all three women (noted in Chapters Five and Six). Though many of these findings were surprising to me to some degree, it has become clearer that this may be the case for most African-American women who are upwardly mobile and no longer live in predominantly Black communities. What I found not to be surprising was that these women grew up in the Black church, which has played a critical role in the social, political, cultural and economic life of most African Americans in this country. As previously noted, Chaka still attends a Black church with her family.

On the one hand, I can relate to these women's experiences walking the halls of the Ivory Tower. Often we are called upon to serve on every committee addressing issues of diversity, or called upon to serve as a mentor for a person of color just because we both fit that category, or sometimes are identified to speak for the "race" as if our voice is the law and has authority to speak for all other African Americans. What then do our lives become when we are positioned in this way? How then do we address the various inequities or injustices that occur without looking like the stereotypical "angry Black woman"? Interestingly, I was asked whether or not I was angry when I responded to a certain question raised by one of the White males on my committee during my defense for my comprehensive exams; this person clearly had misread the passion exuded for the subject matter being discussed. Sometimes the subtle actions of individuals are left alone because their ignorance does not warrant an address; yet, there are other times when it is absolutely necessary to say something or, as I recently heard the Nobel Laureate Toni Morrison say, it may be necessary to "dress them down." As Adjuoa stated in this study, it is sometimes necessary to address the individuals when they are wrong about a particular situation, or sometimes it is absolutely necessary to call them out on addressing various issues.

On the other hand, I would like to raise the question that I have asked many African-American women and possibly offer an alternative way of examining African-American women's leadership in the Academy by the way the women in this study responded to questions about their leadership. The question at the end of the day remains: How do African-American women negotiate their spaces and points of location at a majority institution where institutional practices and systems of domination occur on a day-to-day basis?

The three women in this study have framed their experiences in the Academy, not from a victim's standpoint but from a standpoint of liberation. This perspective is present in the way they articulate their situated identity in the Academy and how they have chosen to deal with their role and responsibilities as deans by serving students, faculty and staff in a way that embodies an ethic of care. The way Adjuoa, Chaka, and Jewel talk about dealing with institutional practices is couched in terms of responding to challenges as opportunities to create change, and as opportunities to creatively look for ways to open up spaces for traditionally marginalized groups. That ethic of care includes developing a path for young scholars entering the Academy by serving as their mentors and assisting in guiding them in the right direction. Embedded within the core of this framework, which stands at the core of their leadership, is their spirituality. For the women in this study, this spirituality serves as an empowering form of resistance when confronted with adversity in various situations.

In advancing the notion of empowering resistance embedded with the framework of African-American women's spirituality, it can be reexamined and likened to Cornel West's (1988) conception of aggressive pessimism. In *Prophetic Fragments*, West (1988) discusses the ways in which African-Americans have sustained themselves despite various forms of institutional and racist practices that have been oppressive to African-American women and men. On the one hand, such oppressive forces have caused many African-Americans to become pessimistic "regarding the possibilities of fundamental transformation of American society and culture."[1] While on the other hand, though, the odds seem so overwhelming, the incorporative strategies of the status quo so effective, along with the racism so deeply entrenched in American life, West (1988) argues that it has not been enough to cause African-Americans to lose hope in their circumstances. In essence, "most prophetic practices among [B]lack Americans have given this pessimism an aggressiveness such that it becomes sobering rather than disenabling, a stumbling block rather than a dead end, a challenge to meet rather than a conclusion to accept."[2] In a similar vein, the women in this study have articulated the way they make meaning of their lives when faced with adversity from a standpoint of hope and accepting the challenge as an opportunity to change things thus allowing their spiritual consciousness to serve as a guide for the way they make decisions and serve others in the Academy. Hence, this spirituality becomes a powerful form of empowering resistance in the lives of Adjuoa, Chaka, and Jewel.

To have an impact on the larger systems of domination which influence the social, political, and cultural construct of higher education, it necessitates the hope, the empowering resistance, the prophetic pessimism embodied by the three women in this study. In turn, this hope, resistance, and prophetic pessimism allows them to continue to withstand various forms of oppression while at the same time addressing ways to create positive change and transformation within the walls of the Ivory Tower. The impact becomes evident when having to address issues regarding various groups of people who have been traditionally marginalized based on race, class, gender or other types of difference. The impact becomes evident when these women maintain their sense of hope and ethical responsibility by not allowing institutional practices to shape their identity but define it for themselves. The impact becomes evident when these women remain standing in the "midst of the storm" continuing to contest the terrain by their mere presence, and individually and collectively asserting their position and voice, ensuring they will be heard on whatever scale, large or small.

The spiritual leadership of these women embodies a sense of hope; yet, embodying an empowering resistance becomes a sustaining force in their everyday leadership practices. This empowering resistance, hence, has played a more critical role in the lives of these three women who have endured the promises and perils of academic life. For the most part, their experiences, like many other African-Americans in the Ivory Tower, can be likened to what W. E. B. Dubois described as the Negro's "double-consciousness" in the beginning of the twentieth century. Dubois' most notable essay, "Of Our Spiritual Strivings," provided an intimate, classic context for describing the plight of one group trying to identify with another group while retaining some of its own characteristics and traditions.[3] Dubois defines this double-consciousness by stating, "One ever feels [her] two-ness, —an American, a Negro; two souls, two thoughts, two unreconciled strivings; two warring ideals in one dark body, whose dogged strength alone keeps it from being torn asunder."[4] As noted by Washington (1997), Dubois could have described the African-American woman as having a third dimension. "She was not only 'born with a veil . . . in this American world,' which yields her no 'true self-consciousness' but allows her to see herself only 'through the revelation of the other world.'"[5] Dubois could have easily spoken of African-American women as possessing a triple consciousness, encompassing her identities as an American, a person of African descent, and a woman. This triple consciousness holds true today for many African-American women in the Ivory Tower.

Despite the triple consciousness that African-American women endure in the Academy, it is their spirituality that has played an important role in shaping and sustaining their lives within an institutionalized system that often ignores their presence and inadvertently attempts to subjugate their leadership role. Like Stewart (1999), it is "African-American spirituality that has an important influence of promoting psychological, spiritual, and physical well-being . . . without spirituality blacks could not attain human wholeness."[6] Hence, African-American spirituality created a balance for a self that was or could have possibly been at war with the larger racial self as well as the anti-self that created psychological ambiguity and self-hatred. Without spirituality's humanizing and radicalizing functions, Blacks would not be able to develop some semblance of spiritual and psychological balance in a dominant culture that has attempted to keep African Americans perpetually off-balance.[7] Furthermore, because African-American spirituality remains one of the humanizing, radicalizing, and holistic forces in the Black experience, it has served as a practice of freedom and enabled African Americans to practice a freedom of expression that directly defies the various processes of devaluation and repression of the larger society. Such freedom is an integral part of African Americans' self-sanity and collective unity. As the women in this study have talked about their spiritual lives and how they make meaning of their leadership, it can be said that their spirituality has served as a practice of freedom which resonates throughout African-American culture; whereas this practice of freedom has been instrumental in the way they interpret, value, express, and construct an existence that reinforces positive norms of self and community.[8] In many ways, the practices of these three African-American women can be seen as having an impact on bridging the gap of the new cultural politics in the Academy as it relates to addressing issues of social justice regarding issues of diversity on college campuses. I would like to go a step further and suggest that their spiritual leadership has served as a framework for helping the dominant group to find a new way of embracing communities of difference. A liberatory praxis would require these institutions to continuously push to address the deep changes within the institution to find ways to embrace communities of difference versus tolerating these differences on college campuses. As we continue to move forward in this new millennium, and in these perilous times, it will cause all of us to take a closer look at how we develop and maintain relationships for a democratic society that can turn the rhetoric of "liberty, and justice for all" into a reality.

At this point, I turn the mirror on myself. In many ways, serving as an "outsider-insider" within this study has continuously caused me to pause. As I have learned and been reassured by the three women in this study that they have not sacrificed their identity as an African-American woman in higher education, I still wonder about the sacrifices that have been made. First, what are the sacrifices and how do they impact their lives on a day-to-day basis? I wonder about this question for many reasons as I begin working full-time in Academia. In walking the halls of the Ivory Tower, what becomes the trade-off for the lives of these women? Beyond what has been mentioned in this study, what in turn are the rewards for the "Adjuoas," "Chakas," and "Jewels" serving in a space that still remains quite traditional and male-centered? Clearly, the spiritual leadership of the women in this study has served as a sustaining force in keeping them centered in their work; but what are the things that have been left unsaid by Adjuoa, Chaka and Jewel? How then are their lives viewed beyond the Academy, especially within the African-American community? What are the pressures placed upon them to "give back" to the African-American community, and how are they called upon to address issues facing Black America? How then will these African-American women's leadership pave the path for future women like myself, leaving a legacy and something to build upon? What does this "building" mean ten to twenty years from now when the current educational system is being overhauled by the "rollback" of Affirmative Action and other policies that directly affect women and people of color? What will become the new mission for African-American women ten to twenty years from now, and how can we proactively begin to envision ways to address these issues? These types of questions remain at the forefront as I try to envision what the future will look like for women and people of color in Academia ten to twenty years from now.

On the other hand, I suggest as a possibility for continuing to create change in the Academy and our communities that the responsibility extends far beyond African-American women. Yes, African-American women do need to maintain a strong sense of consciousness and connectedness in particularly addressing issues of the African-American community, but we must all join hands in transforming the world for the success and sustainability of generations to come. This transformation requires all groups of people, regardless of race, class, gender and various other types of difference, to call into question their own spirit. It requires a shift in conscience and consciousness. In shifting the paradigm, it requires individuals to "carry a sense of responsibility for correcting the injustices of the past; for understanding how and why atrocities are committed; and it must include a means for avoiding repetition of past crimes . . . there must be a willingness and an ability to imagine ourselves as *different Beings*, and from that imagining to think and act differently."[9]

Then, as our foremother Mary McLeod Bethune stated in "My Last Will and Testament" (1955), to the women and men of African descent, her words still resonate as we continue to explore and find new ways to change the world in the twenty-first century. The African-American community is still faced with many challenges in teaching our children. Here are some of Bethune's (1999) words of wisdom that she has left behind:

> I leave you love . . . I leave you hope . . . I leave you the challenge of developing confidence in one another . . . I leave you a thirst for education . . . I leave you a respect for the uses of power . . . I leave you faith . . . I leave you racial dignity . . . I leave you a desire to live harmoniously with your fellow men [and women] . . . I leave you finally a responsibility to young people . . . . We have a powerful potential

> in our youth, and we must have the courage to change old ideas and practices so that we may direct their power toward good ends.
>
> Faith, courage, brotherhood [and sisterhood], dignity, ambition, responsibility—these are needed today as never before. We must cultivate them and use them as tools for our task of completing the establishment of equality for the [African-American and other marginalized groups of people]. We must sharpen the tools in the struggle that faces us and find new ways of using them. The Freedom Gates are half ajar. We must pry them fully open.[10]

The words of Mary McLeod Bethune still hold true today; though we have won many battles we still have other challenges facing us, and we cannot afford to forget these words, as we pave the path and pass the torch for our young people coming behind us. Clearly, the legacy of our foremothers, the contemporary women's stories, and the spiritual nature of their lives pushes us to continue to think about new ways to build bridges, bring borders together, and harmonize in our differences to bring forth change for us all in a country that is seeking more of the "Spirit" than solely relying upon one's own capacity to make that change.

APPENDIX A
Letter to Prospective Participants

Rochelle Garner
xxxxxxxx
xxxxxxxx

October 18, 2000

Dear

Thank you for allowing me the opportunity to share information with you about my dissertation research topic on The Spiritual Leadership of African-American Women in the Academy. I have included a brief synopsis of my intent, along with questions I would raise to better understand how spirituality is interwoven into the fabric of African- American women's leadership. Though this study may be generalizable in many ways, I realize that it is not applicable to all African-American women in administrative roles.

- **Purpose:** In this study, I propose to examine the lives of African-American women in leadership in the academy, and how spirituality has shaped their lives and influenced their leadership. Spirituality has not only served as a source of strength and empowerment in African-American women's leadership, but I also believe it has served as a form of empowering resistance. Thus, what are the ways African- American women have used their spirituality as a lens to lead, and how does this leadership impact the social, cultural, and political construct in a male-dominated arena?

- **Interview Questions:**

1. Please describe your career path?
2. Name five adjectives to describe your leadership?
3. Which societal organization(s) or institution(s) have helped to shape/influence who you are today?
4. What is the significance of spirituality in your life? If any?
5. How do you define spirituality?
6. In what ways has your spirituality played a role in shaping who you are as a leader?
7. Name a moral or ethical dilemma you have encountered in your position (current or past), and how did you choose to resolve the issue?
8. What "guides" do you use in making your decisions — (e.g. personal belief system, communal codes, professional rules, legal rules, etc.)?
9. In what ways have you had to deal with adversity as a female administrator, and how were you able to overcome these challenges?
10. How have you been able to develop a sense of community at your university?
11. What types of support systems have you created which serve as buffers in order to deal with the day-to-day challenges of being a college president?
12. What do you find most rewarding about your position?

- **Interview Process:** This will consist of a three-part series. The first interview will focus more specifically on your life history. The second interview will look at the details of your present leadership experience and more specifically get into the details of the topic area of study. The third interview will reflect more clearly on the "meaning " of your leadership experience.

In analyzing and interpreting the data, I will use a constant comparative method by looking at key words and phrases, and emerging themes. I will also conduct a "member check" allowing each participant to review the data and how it has been recorded. More importantly, each person's name in this study will be kept confidential by using pseudonyms chosen by the participant.

I recognize your demanding schedule and would be willing to work around your schedule as much as possible. Upon receipt of this letter, I will follow-up with a phone call to confirm receipt of this information, and to discuss how we may possibly work together on this research study. I would be interested in answering any questions you may have of me. If you have any immediate questions, you may contact me via email: garnerr@muohio.edu.

In advance, I appreciate your willingness to talk with me and hopefully I will gain a commitment of us working together on this exciting project.

Sincerely,

Rochelle Garner

Notes

SETTING THE CONTEXT

1. Ecc. 9. 11 King James Version.
2. Clifford Geertz, *The Interpretation of Cultures* (New York: Basic Books, Inc. Publishers, 1973), 127.
3. Geneva Smitherman, *Talkin and Testifyin: The Language of Black America* (Detroit: Wayne State University Press, 1977), 103.
4. Gene McFadden and John Whitehead, "Ain't No Stoppin' Us Now" in *McFadden and Whitehead*, Capitol Records, B000006LA7.

CHAPTER 1. WHEN AND WHERE WE ENTER THE ACADEMY

1. Michael I. N. Dash, Jonathon Jackson and Stephen Rasor, *Hidden Wholeness: An African-American Spirituality for Individuals and Communities* (Cleveland OH; United Church Press, 1997), 93.
2. Joanne E. Cooper, "Telling Our Own Stories: The Reading and Writing of Journals or Diaries", in *Stories Lives Tell: Narrative and Dialogue in Education*, edited by Carol Witherell and Nel Noddings (New York: Teachers College Press, 1991), 111.
3. Alexander W. Astin and Astin S. Astin, *Meaning and Spirituality in the*

   Lives of College Faculty: A Study of Values, Authenticity, and Stress, Higher Education Research Institute, University of California, Los Angeles, 1999, 1.
4. Carlyle F. Stewart, *Black Spirituality and Black Consciousness: Soul Force, Culture and Freedom in the African-American Experience* (Trenton, N.J.: Africa World Press, Inc., 1999), 6–7.
5. Stewart, 7.
6. Dash et al, 95.

7. Dash et al, 95.

8. Manning Marable and Leith Mullings, eds. *Let Nobody Turn Us Around: Voices of Resistance, Reform and Renewal* (Lanham MD: Rowman and Littlefield Publishers, Inc., 2000), 114.

9. Katie Cannon, *Katie's Canon: Womanism and the Soul of the Black Community* (New
York: The Continuum Publishing Company 1995), 33.

10. Cannon, 35.

11. Cannon, 33.

12. Cannon, 33

13. Cannon, 33.

14. Cannon, 34.

15. Petra Munro, *Subject to Fiction: Women Teachers' Life History Narratives and the Cultural Politics of Resistance* (Philadelphia: Open University Press, 1998), 31.

16. Bettina Aptheker, *Tapestries of Life* (Amherst, MA: University of Massachusetts Press, 1989),173.

17. Munro, 31.

18. Sounds of Blackness, "Hold On," on *Africa to America: The Journey of the Drum*, Sounds of Blackness, Perspective Records compact disc, B0000012SX.

19. Mary Mary, "Shackles," on *Thankful*, Mary Mary, Sony Music Entertainment, Inc. compact disc, B00004T0Q1.

20. Patricia H. Collins, *Fighting Words: Black Women and the Search for Justice* (Minneapolis: University of Minnesota Press, 1998), 229.

21. Sonia Sanchez, quoted in Collins, 247.

22. Marimba Ani, *Let the Circle be Unbroken: The Implications of African Spirituality in the Diaspora* (New York: Nkonimfo Publications, 1980), 41.

23. Moira Ferguson, ed., *The History of Mary Prince, a West Indian Slave: Related by Herself* (Ann Arbor, MI: University of Michigan Press, 1993), 60.

24. James D. Anderson, *The Education of Blacks in the South, 1860–1935* (Chapel Hill, NC: University of North Carolina Press, 1988), 7.

25. Anderson, 7.

26. Karen Ann Johnson, *Uplifting the Women and the Race: The Educational Philosophies and Social Activism of Anna Julia Cooper and Nannie Helen Burroughs* (New York: Garland Publishing, Inc., 2000), 23.

27. Johnson, 23.

28. Johnson, 23.

29. Johnson, 24.

30. Darlene Clark Hine and Kathleen Thompson, *A Shining Thread of*

Hope: The History of Black Women in America (New York: Broadway Books, 1998),123.

31. Hine and Thompson, 182.
32. Hine and Thompson, 184.
33. Anderson, 238.
34. Anderson, 238.
35. Anderson, 239.
36. Anderson, 239.
37. Nellie McKay, "A Troubled Peace: Black Women in the Halls of the White Academy" in *Black Women in the Academy: Promises and Perils*, ed. Lois Benjamin (Gainesville, FL: University Press of Florida, 1997), 13.
38. McKay, 13.
39. Linda M. Perkins, "Lucy Diggs Slowe: Champion of the Self-Determination of African-American Women in Higher Education," *Journal of Negro History* (1996): 90.
40. Perkins, 90.
41. Elizabeth L. Ihle, "Lucy Diggs Slowe," in *Women Educators in the United States, 1820–1993: A Bio-Bibliographical Sourcebook*, ed. Maxine Schwartz Seller (Westport, CT: Greenwood Press, 1994), 447.
42. Ihle, 447.
43. Ihle, 448.
44. Ihle, 448.
45. Ihle, 448.
46. Ihle, 451.
47. Perkins, 93.
48. Perkins, 92.
49. Perkins, 92.
50. Perkins, 93.
51. Perkins, 99.
52. Patricia Bell-Scott, "To Keep My Self-Respect: Dean Lucy Diggs Slowe's Memorandum on the Sexual Harassment of Black Women," *NWSA Journal* 9 (1997): 70–76.
53. Ihle, 452.
54. Charles Lemert and Esme Bhan, eds. *The Voice of Julia Ann Cooper* (Lanham, MD: Rowman and Littlefield Publishers, Inc. 1998), 345.
55. Beverly Guy-Sheftall, "Anna Julia Cooper," in *Women Educators in the United States, 1820–1993: A Bio-Bibliographical Sourcebook*, ed. Maxine S. Seller (Westport, CT: Greenwood Press, 1994), 161–67.
56. Lemert and Bhan, 7.
57. Lemert and Bhan, 8.
58. Guy-Sheftall, 162.
59. Guy-Sheftall, 162.

60. Guy-Sheftall, 163.
61. Guy Sheftall, 163.
62. Lemert and Bhan, 10.
63. Lemert and Bhan, 10.
64. Lemert and Bhan, 11.
65. Guy-Sheftall, 165.
66. Guy-Sheftall, 165.
67. Audrey Thomas McCluskey, "Most Sacrificing Service: The Educational Leadership of Lucy Craft Laney and Mary McLeod Bethune," in *Women of the South: A Multicultural Reader*, ed. Christie Ann Farnham (New York: New York University Press, 1997), 196.
68. Audrey Thomas McCluskey and Elaine Smith, *Mary McLeod Bethune: Building a Better World* (Bloomington, IN: Indiana University Press, 1999), 5.
69. McCluskey, 197.
70. McCluskey and Smith, 5.
71. Hine and Thompson, 250.
72. McCluskey and Smith, 6.
73. McCluskey and Smith, 8.
74. McCluskey and Smith, 8.
75. McCluskey and Smith, 9.

CHAPTER 2. SURVEYING THE LITERATURE

1. Patricia H. Collins, *Black Feminist Thought: Knowledge, Consciousness, and the Politics of Empowerment*, 2nd ed. (New York: Routledge, 2000), 215.
2. Collins 2000, 39.
3. bell hooks, *Teaching to Transgress: Education as the Practice of Freedom* (New York: Routledge, 1994), 22.
4. hooks, 23.
5. Collins 2000, 35.
6. Patricia Reid-Merritt, *Sister Power: How Phenomenal Black Women are Rising to the Top* (New York: J. Wiley, 1996).
7. Mary S. Hartman, *Talking Leadership: Conversations with Powerful Women* (New Brunswick, NJ, Rutgers University Press), 1.
8. Ruth J. Simmons, quoted in Hartman, 253.
9. Gilbert W. Fairholm, *Capturing the Heart of Leadership: Spirituality and Community in the new American Workplace* (Westport, CT: Praeger Publishers, 1997), x.
10. Fairholm, x.
11. Robert J. Starratt, *The Drama of Leadership* (London: The Falmer Press, 1993), 41.

12. Starratt, 41.
13. Gareth Morgan, *Images of Organization*, 2nd ed. (Thousand Oaks, CA: Sage Publications, 1997), 102.
14. Morgan, 138.
15. Morgan, 141.
16. Morgan, 166.
17. Sally Helgesen, *The Female Advantage: Women's Ways of Leadership* (New York: Doubleday, 1995), 31.
18. Helgesen, 40.
19. Estela Mara Bensimon and Anna Neumann, *Redesigning Collegiate Leaders: Teams and Teamwork in Higher Education* (Baltimore: The Johns Hopkins University Press, 1993), 19.
20. Collins 2000, 33.
21. Collins 2000, 34.
22. Collins 2000, 34.
23. Richard Quantz, "On Critical Ethnography (with Some Postmodern Considerations)," in *The Handbook of Qualitative Research*, eds. Margaret LeCompte, Wendy L. Millroy and Judith Preissle, (San Diego, CA: Academic Press, Inc., 1992), 487.
24. Quantz, 487.
25. bell hooks, *Talking Back: Thinking Feminist, Thinking Black* (Boston: South End Press, 1989), 24.
26. Quantz, 487.
27. hooks 1989, 24.
28. Collins 2000, 39.
29. Collins 2000, 35.
30. Collins 2000, 35.
31. Collins 2000, 39.
32. Collins 2000, 215.
33. Collins 2000, 39.
34. hooks 1989, 22.
35. hooks, 1989, 23.
36. Collins 2000, 35.
37. Peter J. Paris, *The Spirituality of African Peoples: The Search for a Common Moral Discourse* (Minneapolis: Fortress Press, 1995), 44.
38. Paris, 44–5.
39. Parker J. Palmer, *Leading from Within: Reflections on Spirituality and Leadership* (Washington, DC: Servant Leadership Press, 1999), 3.
40. Robert Quinn, *Deep Change* (San Francisco: Jossey-Bass Publishers, 1996), 5.
41. Quinn, 11.
42. Quinn, 9.
43. Janet O. Hagberg, *Real Power: Stages of Personal Power in*

Organizations (Salem, WI: Sheffield Publishing Company, 1994), 227.

44. Hagberg, 227–8.
45. Hagberg, 228.
46. Hagberg, 228.
47. Bensimon and Newmann, xv.
48. Judy Rogers, *Leadership as Spiritual Journey* (Oxford, OH: Miami University Press, 1999), 3.
49. Rogers, 3.
50. Rogers, 3–4.
51. Hagberg, 230.
52. Hagberg, 230.
53. Hagberg, 259.
54. Hagberg, 259–60.

CHAPTER 3. METHODOLOGY

1. Robert E. Stake, Case Studies, in *Handbook of Qualitative Research*, eds. Norman K. Denzin and Yvonna S. Lincoln (Thousand Oaks, CA: Sage Publications, 1994), 236.
2. Collins 2000, 35.
3. Collins 2000, 35.
4. hooks 1989, 42–3.
5. Teresa Fry Brown, *God Don't Like Ugly: African-American Women Handing Down Spiritual Values* (Nashville, TN: Abingdon Press, 2000), 103.
6. Munro, 5.
7. Carol Christ, quoted in Munro, 5.
8. Munro, 5.
9. Linda Thompson, "Feminist Methodology for Family Studies," *Journal of Marriage and the Family*, 54, no. 1 (1992): 9.
10. Thompson, 10.
11. Thompson, 10.
12. Margaret D. LeCompte and Judith Preissle. *Ethnography and Qualitative Design in Educational Research*, 2nd ed. (San Diego, CA: Academic Press, 1993), 168.
13. Dickens and Fontana, 209.
14. Irving Seidman, *Interviewing as Qualitative Research: A Guide for Researchers in Education and the Social Sciences* (New York: Teachers College Press, 1998), 3.
15. Course Instructor's Name, Class Handout, EDL 775, Educational Leadership Department, Miami University, Oxford, OH, March 4, 1999.
16. Quantz, 473.
17. Seidman, 12.

18. Seidman, 12.
19. Seidman, 29.
20. LeCompte and Preissle, 224.

CHAPTER 5. THE SOULS OF MY SISTERS: TALKIN' AND TESTIFYIN'

1. Fairholm, 80.
2. Collins 2000, 264.
3. hooks, 1994, 13.
4. Palmer, 11.
5. Mic. 6. 8 King James Version.
6. Max De Pree, Leadership Jazz (New York: Dell Publishing, 1992), 126.
7. Collins 2000, 35.
8. L. A. Napier, "The Moral Journey Toward Purpose: The Importance of Self-Exploration Before Choosing to Lead," in *School Leadership: Expanding Horizons of the Mind and Spirit*, eds. L. T. Fenwick and P. Jenkins (Lancaster, PA: Technomic Publishing Co., 1999), 17.
9. R. M. Brewer, "Giving Name and Voice: Black Women Scholars, Research, and Knowledge Transformation," in *Black Women in the Academy: Promises and Perils*, ed. Lois Benjamin (Gainesville, FL: University Press of Florida, 1997), 76.
10. Herb Boyd, *Autobiography of a People: Three Centuries of African-American History Told by Those Who Lived It* (New York: Doubleday, 2000), 1.
11. Fairholm, x.

CHAPTER 6. STILL LIFTING AS WE CLIMB

1. Collins 2000, 177.
2. Khaula Murtadha-Watts, "Spirited Sisters: Spirituality and the Activism of African-American Women in Educational Leadership," in *School Leadership: Expanding Horizons of the Mind and Spirit*, eds. L. T. Fenwick and P. Jenkins (Lancaster, PA; Technomic Publishing Co., 1999),156.
3. Napier, 18.
4. Robert Heifetz, *Leadership Without Easy Answers* (Cambridge, MA: The Belknap Press of Harvard University Press, 1998),18.
5. Fairholm, 80.
6. Fairholm, 198.
7. Fairholm, 198.
8. Fairholm, 198.
9. Heifetz, 21.

10. Collins 2000, 264.
11. Collins 200, 263.
12. Quinn, 34–5.
13. Mic. 6. 8
14. Collins 2000, 189.
15. Collins 2000, 191.
16. Collins 2000, 210.
17. Stanlie M. James and Abena P. A. Busia, eds., *Theorizing Black Feminism: The Visionary Pragmatism of Black Women* (New York: Routledge, 1993), 47.
18. James and Busia, 48.
19. bell hooks 1989, 149.
20. bell hooks 1989, 150–1.
21. Heifetz, 185.
22. Palmer, 2.
23. Palmer, 2.
24. Palmer, 2.
25. C. L. Larson and Khaula Murtadha, "title of the paper read at the conference," paper presented at city, state, month, year, 2–3.
26. Ngugi Wa Thiong'O, *Decolonizing the Mind: The Politics of Language in African Literature* (London: Heinemann Press, 1986), 4.
27. Henry A. Giroux, *Border Crossings: Cultural Workers and the Politics of Education* (New York: Routledge, 1993), 19.
28. Giroux, 19.
29. Fairholm, 133.
30. Fairholm, 133.
31. Kimberly Springer, ed., *Still Lifting, Still Climbing: African-American Women's Contemporary Activism* (New York: New York University Press, 1999), 2.
32. Springer, 3.
33. Springer, 3.
34. Josie R. Johnson, "An African-American Female Senior-Level Adminisrator: Facing the Challenges of a Major Research University," in *Black Women in the Academy: Promises and Perils*, ed. Lois Benjamin (Gainesville, FL: University of Florida Press, 1997), 279.
35. Stewart, 43.
36. Stewart, 42.
37. Stewart, 43.
38. Stewart, 43.
39. Aaronette M. White, "Talking Black, Talking Feminist: Gendered Micro-Mobilization Processes in a Collective Protest Against Rape," in *Still Lifting, Still Climbing: African-American Women's Contemporary Activism* , ed. Kimberly Springer (New York: New York University Press, 1999), 190.

CHAPTER 7. OF OUR SPIRITUAL STRIVINGS

1. Cornel West, *Prophetic Fragments* (Grand Rapids, MI: William B. Eerdmans Publishing Co. and Trenton, NJ: Africa World Press, Inc., 1988), 42.

2. West. 42.

3. Delo E. Washington, "Another Voice from the Wilderness," in *Black Women in the Academy: Promises and Perils*, ed. Lois Benjamin. (Gainesville, FL: University of Florida Press, 1997), 275.

4. David Levering Lewis, ed., *W.E.B. Dubois: A Reader* (Henry Holt and Company, LLC., 1995), 29.

5. Washington, 275.

6. Stewart, 43.

7. Stewart, 43.

8. Stewart, 42.

9. M. J. Ryan, ed., *The Fabric of the Future: Women Visionaries Illuminate the Path to Tomorrow* (Berkeley, CA: Conari Press, 1998), 75.

10. Mary McLeod Bethune, "My Last Will and Testament," in *Mary McLeod Bethune: Building a Better World*, ed. Audrey McCluskey and Elaine Smith. (Bloomington, IN: Indiana University Press,1999), 61.

Bibliography

Anderson, James D. *The Education of Blacks in the South, 1860–1935.* Chapel Hill, NC: University of North Carolina Press, 1988.

Ani, Marimba. *Let the Circle be Unbroken: The Implications of African Spirituality in the Diaspora.* New York: Nkonimfo Publications,1980.

Aptheker, Bettina. *Tapestries of Life.* Amherst, MA: University of Massachusetts Press, 1989.

Asante, Molefi Kete. *The Afrocentric Idea.* Amherst, MA: University of Massachusetts Press, 1998.

Astin, Alexander W. and Astin S. Astin. *Meaning and Spirituality in the Lives of College Faculty: A Study of Values, Authenticity, an Stress.* Higher Education Research Institute, University of California. Los Angeles, 1999.

Bell-Scott, Patricia. "To Keep My Self-Respect: Dean Lucy Diggs Slowe's Memorandum on the Sexual Harassment of Black Women." *NWSA Journal* 9 (1997): 70–76.

Bell-Scott, Patricia and Juanita Johnson-Bailey. *Flat-Footed Truths: Telling Black Women's Lives.* New York: Henry Holt & Company, Inc., 1998.

Benjamin, Lois. *Black Women in the Academy: Promises and Perils.* Gainesville, FL: University of Florida Press, 1997.

Bensimon, Estela Mara and Anna Neumann. *Redesigning Collegiate Leaders: Teams and Teamwork in Higher Education.* Baltimore: The Johns Hopkins University Press, 1993.

Boyd, Herb. *Autobiography of a People: Three Centuries of African-American History Told by Those Who Lived It.* New York: Doubleday, 2000.

Brewer, Rose M. "Giving Name and Voice: Black Women Scholars,

Research, and Knowledge Transformation." In *Black Women in the Academy: Promises and Perils*, ed. Lois Benjamin. Gainesville, FL: University Press of Florida, 1997.

Brown, Teresa Fry. *God Don't Like Ugly: African-American Women Handing Down Spiritual Values*. Nashville, TN: Abingdon Press, 2000.

Cannon, Katie. *Katie's Canon: Womanism and the Soul of the Black Community*. New York: The Continuum Publishing Company, 1995.

Collins, Patricia H. *Fighting Words: Black Women and the Search for Justice*. Minneapolis: University of Minnesota Press, 1998.

Collins, Patricia H. *Black Feminist Thought: Knowledge, Consciousness, and the Politics of Empowerment*, 2nd ed. New York: Routledge, 2000.

Cooper, Joanne E. "Telling Our Own Stories: The Reading and Writing of Journals or Diaries." In *Stories Lives Tell: Narrative and Dialogue in Education*, edited by Carol Witherell and Nel Noddings. New York: Teachers College Press, 1991.

Dash, Michael I. N., Jonathon Jackson and Stephen Rasor. *Hidden Wholeness: An African-American Spirituality for Individuals and Communities*. Cleveland OH; United Church Press, 1997.

De Pree, Max. *Leadership Jazz*. New York: Dell Publishing, 1992.

Dickens and Fontana. 1994.

Ephirim-Donkor, Anthony. *African Spirituality: On Becoming Ancestors*. Trenton, NJ: African World Press, 1997.

Fairholm, Gilbert W. *Capturing the Heart of Leadership: Spirituality and Community in the New American Workplace*. Westport, CT: Praeger Publishers, 1997.

Farnham, Christie Anne. *Women in the American South: A Multicultural Reader*. New York: New York University Press, 1997.

Geertz, Clifford. *The Interpretation of Cultures*. New York: Basic Books, Inc. Publishers, 1973.

Giroux, Henry A. *Border Crossings: Cultural Workers and the Politics of Education*. New York: Routledge, 1993.

Guy-Sheftall, Beverly. "Anna Julia Cooper." In *Women Educators in the United States, 1820–1993: A Bio-Bibliographical Sourcebook*, edited by Maxine S. Seller. Westport, CT: Greenwood Press, 1994.

Guy-Sheftall, Beverly, ed. *Words of Fire: An Anthology of African-American Feminist Thought*. New York: The New Press, 1995.

Hagberg, Janet O. *Real Power: Stages of Personal Power in Organizations*. Salem, WI: Sheffield Publishing Company, 1994.

Hartman, Mary S. *Talking Leadership: Conversations with Powerful Women*. New Brunswick, NJ: Rutgers University Press, 1999.

Heifetz, Robert. *Leadership Without Easy Answers*. Cambridge, MA: The Belknap Press of Harvard University Press, 1998.

Helgesen, Sally. *The Female Advantage: Women's Ways of Leadership*. New York: Doubleday, 1995.

Hine, Darlene Clark and Kathleen Thompson. *A Shining Thread of Hope: The History of Black Women in America*. New York: Broadway Books, 1998.

hooks, bell. *Feminist Theory: From Margin to Center*. Boston: South End Press, 1984.

hooks, bell. *Talking Back: Thinking Feminist, Thinking Black*. Boston: South End Press, 1989.

hooks, bell. *Teaching to Transgress: Education as the Practice of Freedom*. New York: Routledge, 1994.

Hull, Akasha Gloria. *The New Spirituality of African-American Women*. Rochester, VT: Inner Traditions International, 2001.

Ihle, Elizabeth L. "Lucy Diggs Slowe." In *Women Educators in the United States, 1820 1993: A Bio-Bibliographical Sourcebook*, edited by Maxine S. Seller. Westport, CT: Greenwood Press, 1994.

James, Stanlie M. and Abena P. A. Busia, eds. *Theorizing Black Feminism: The Visionary Pragmatism of Black Women*. New York: Routledge, 1993.

Johnson, Josie R. "An African-American Female Senior-Level Administrator: Facing the Challenges of a Major Research University." In *Black Women in the Academy: Promises and Perils*, edited by Lois Benjamin. Gainesville, FL: University of Florida Press, 1997.

Johnson, Karen Ann. *Uplifting the Women and the Race: The Educational Philosophies and Social Activism of Anna Julia Cooper and Nannie Helen Burroughs*. New York: Garland Publishing, Inc., 2000.

Larson, C. L. and Khaula Murtadha, "Leadership for Social Justice." Paper presented at the Annual UCEA Conference, Cincinnati, OH, November, 2001.

LeCompte, Margaret D. and Judith Preissle. *Ethnography and Qualitative Design in Educational Research*, 2nd ed. San Diego, CA: Academic Press, 1993.

Lemert, Charles and Esme Bhan, eds. *The Voice of Julia Ann Cooper*. Lanham, MD: Rowman and Littlefield Publishers, Inc., 1998.

Lewis, David Levering, ed. *W.E.B. Dubois: A Reader*. Henry Holt and

Company, LLC., 1995.

Marable, Manning and Leith Mullings, eds. *Let Nobody Turn Us Around: Voices of Resistance, Reform and Renewal.* Lanham MD: Rowman and Littlefield Publishers, Inc., 2000.

McLeod Bethune, Mary. "My Last Will and Testament." In *Mary McLeod Bethune: Building a Better World.* Edited by Audrey McCluskey and Elaine Smith. Bloomington, IN: Indiana University Press,1999.

McCluskey, Audrey Thomas. "Most Sacrificing Service: The Educational Leadership of Lucy Craft Laney and Mary McLeod Bethune." In *Women of the South: A Multicultural Reader*, edited by Christie Ann Farnham. New York: New York University Press, 1997.

McCluskey, Audrey Thomas and Elaine Smith. *Mary McLeod Bethune: Building a Better World.* Bloomington, IN: Indiana University Press, 1999.

McKay, Nellie. "A Troubled Peace: Black Women in the Halls of the White Academy." In *Black Women in the Academy: Promises and Perils*, edited by Lois Benjamin. Gainesville, FL: University Press of Florida, 1997.

Morgan, Gareth. *Images of Organization*, 2nd ed. Thousand Oaks, CA: Sage Publications, 1997.

Munro, Petra. *Subject to Fiction: Women Teachers' Life History Narratives and the Cultural Politics of Resistance.* Philadelphia: Open University Press, 1998.

Murtadha-Watts, Khaula. "Spirited Sisters: Spirituality and the Activism of African American Women in Educational Leadership." In *School Leadership: Expanding Horizons of the Mind and Spirit*, edited by L. T. Fenwick and P. Jenkins. Lancaster, PA; Technomic Publishing Co., 1999.

Napier, L. A. "The Moral Journey Toward Purpose: The Importance of Self-Exploration Before Choosing to Lead." In *School Leadership: Expanding Horizons of theMind and Spirit*, edited by Leslie T. Fenwick and Patrick Jenkins. Lancaster, PA: Technomic Publishing Co., 1999.

Palmer, Parker J. *Leading from Within: Reflections on Spirituality and Leadership.* Washington, DC: Servant Leadership Press, 1999.

Paris, Peter J. *The Spirituality of African Peoples: The Search for a Common Moral Discourse.* Minneapolis: Fortress Press, 1995.

Perkins, Linda M. "Lucy Diggs Slowe: Champion of the Self Determination of African American Women in Higher Education." *Journal of Negro History* 81 (1996): 89 104.

Prince, Mary. *The History of Mary Prince, a West Indian Slave: Related by*

Herself. Edited by Moira Ferguson. Ann Arbor, MI: University of Michigan Press, 1993.

Quantz, Richard. "On Critical Ethnography (with Some Postmodern Considerations)." In *The Handbook of Qualitative Research*, edited by Margaret LeCompte, Wendy L. Millroy and Judith Preissle. San Diego, CA: Academic Press, Inc., 1992.

Quinn, Robert. *Deep Change*. San Francisco: Jossey-Bass Publishers, 1996.

Reid-Merritt, Patricia. *Sister Power: How Phenomenal Black Women are Rising to the Top*. New York: J. Wiley, 1996.

Rogers, Judy. *Leadership as a Spiritual Journey*. Unpublished Paper. Oxford, OH: Miami University, 1999.

Royster, Jacqueline Jones. *Traces of a Stream: Literacy and Social Change Among African-American Women*. Pittsburgh PA: University of Pittsburgh Press, 2000.

Ryan, M. J., ed. *The Fabric of the Future: Women Visionaries Illuminate the Path to Tomorrow*. Berkeley, CA: Conari Press, 1998.

Seidman, Irving. *Interviewing as Qualitative Research: A Guide for Researchers in Education and the Social Sciences*. New York: Teachers College Press, 1998.

Seller, Maxine Schwartz. *Women Educators in the United States, 1820–1993: A Bio Bibliographical Sourcebook*. Westport, CT.: Greenwood Press,1994.

Smitherman, Geneva. *Talkin and Testifyin: The Language of Black America*. Detroit: Wayne State University Press, 1977.

Sounds of Blackness, "Hold On." On *Africa to America: The Journey of the Drum*. Sounds of Blackness. Perspective Records compact disc, 1994.

Springer, Kimberly, ed. *Still Lifting, Still Climbing: African-American Women's Contemporary Activism*. New York: New York University Press, 1999.

Stake, Robert E. Case Studies. In *Handbook of Qualitative Research*, edited by Norman K. Denzin and Yvonna S. Lincoln. Thousand Oaks, CA: Sage Publications, 1994.

Starratt, Robert J. *The Drama of Leadership*. London: The Falmer Press, 1993.

Stewart, Carlyle F. *Black Spirituality and Black Consciousness: Soul Force, Culture and Freedom in the African-American Experience*. Trenton, N.J.: Africa World Press, Inc., 1999.

Thompson, Linda. "Feminist Methodology for Family Studies." *Journal of*

Marriage and the Family, 54, no. 1 (1992): 3–18.

Wa Thiong'O, Ngugi. *Decolonizing the Mind: The Politics of Language in African Literature*. London: Heinemann Press, 1986.

Washington, Delo E. "Another Voice from the Wilderness." In *Black Women in the Academy: Promises and Perils*, edited by Lois Benjamin. Gainesville, FL: University of Florida Press, 1997.

West, Cornel. *Prophetic Fragments*. Grand Rapids, MI: William B. Eerdmans Publishing Co. and Trenton, NJ: Africa World Press, Inc., 1988.

White, Aaronette M. "Talking Black, Talking Feminist: Gendered Micro Mobilization Processes in a Collective Protest Against Rape." In *Still Lifting, Still Climbing: African-American Women's Contemporary Activism*, edited by Kimberly Springer. New York: New York University Press, 1999.

Index

A

Activism, 91
Adjuoa
  community activism by, 77-78, 90
  education of, 51, 73
  ethic of care, 69-72
  interview with, 48-52, 73
  leadership style of, 64-65, 73
  as mentor, 83
  spirituality of, 51
  spiritually guided leadership of, 64-65, 80, 89
African-American women
  community and, 50-51, 95-96
  educators, 12-21
  higher education for, 10-12
  socio-historical framework of, 5-10
  spirituality of, 4-5, 7
  as teachers, 11
African humanism, 24
African spirituality, 31-32
Aggressive pessimism, 97
Alpha Kappa Alpha Sorority, 13
Alpha Phi Literary Society, 13
Anderson, J.D., 10, 12
Ani, M., 9, 31, 82
Aptheker, B., 7
Astin, A.S., 4
Astin, A.W., 4

B

Baumfree, I., 8
Bell-Scott, P., 47
Benjamin, L., 24, 25, 40
Bennett College, 11
Bensimon, E.M., 24, 27, 28
Bethune, M.M., 19-21, 76, 79, 100-101
Bethune-Cookman College, 20
Bhan, E., 17, 18
Black church, 11-12, 58, 96
Black colleges, 11
Brewer, R.M., 76
Brown, T.F., 38
Bundles, A., xvii
Busia, A.P.A., 24, 40, 84, 85

C

"Call-response", xvii
Cannon, K., 6, 7
Caring. *See* Ethic of care
Chaka
  community activism by, 77, 90-91
  education of, 59-60
  ethic of care, 67-69

ethical issues and, 75
interview with, 57-61, 73
leadership style of, 66-67, 80, 81, 88
as mentor, 84, 86
spirituality of, 58, 96
spiritually guided leadership of, 66-67, 80, 89
Christ, C., 38
Church. *See* Black church; Spirituality
Collins, P.H., 7, 8, 24, 28, 30, 38, 40, 67, 72-73, 79, 82, 84, 85
Community, African Americans and, 50-51, 95-96
Community activism
by Adjuoa, 77-78, 90
by Chaka, 77, 90-91
by Jewel, 76-77, 91
leadership and, 90-92
Conference of Deans and Advisors of Women of Colored Schools, 15
Cookman Institute, 20
Cooper, A.J., 3, 13, 17-19, 21, 30, 76
Coppin, F., 13
Cultural community, 50-51

D

Dash, M.I.N., 5, 31
Daytona Educational and Industrial School for Negro Girls, 20
Deveaux, 10
"Direct action", 91
"Double consciousness", 98
Dress style, 49
Dubois, W.E.B., 98
Durkee, J.S., 14, 16

E

Education
for African-American women, history of, 10-12
morality and, 11
Educators
profiles of, 12-21
See also Teachers
Empowering resistance, 8-10
Ephirim-Donkor, A., 24
Ethic of care, 67-72, 82-87
of Adjuoa, 69-72
of Chaka, 67-69
mentoring, 83-84
"othermothering", 83-86
Ethics, leadership and, 72-73

F

Fairholm, G.W., 24, 25-26, 28, 64-65, 78, 81, 89
Farnham, C.A.
Feminist/womanist theory, xviii, 24, 28-31
women's research and, 37-41
Fisk University, 11
Folktales, 6
Frelinghuysen University, 18

G

Giroux, H.A., 88
God, African view of, 31-32
God-talk, 42, 79, 94
Grandmothers, xiv-xvii
Grassroots politics of feminism, 29
Guy-Sheftall, B., 17, 19, 24

H

Hagberg, J.O., 33-34
Haines Institute, 19
Hairstyles, 49
Hamer, F.L., 30
Hampton Institute, 11
Harper, F.W., 13

Havel, V., 87
Heifetz, R., 24
Helgesen, S., 24, 25, 27, 28
Hine, D.C., 11
hooks, b., 24, 29, 30, 37, 38, 40, 71-72
Hopkins, 24
Hull, A.G., 31

I

Ihle, E.L., 14, 16
Institutional practices, 97

J

Jackson, J., 5, 31
James, S.M., 24, 40, 84, 85
Jewel
  community activism by, 76-77, 91
  education of, 54
  interview with, 52-57, 73
  leadership style of, 55, 74-75
  as mentor, 86-87
  spirituality of, 55-57
  spiritually guided leadership of, 65-66, 80, 89
Johnson, J.R., 92
Johnson, K.A., 11, 17
Johnson, M., 16, 20-21
Johnson-Bailey, J.

L

Laney, L.C., 19-20
Language, 9
Larson, C.L., 88
Leadership
  by Adjuoa, 64-65, 73
  by Chaka, 66-67, 80, 81, 88
  community activism and, 90-92
  definition of, 34
  ethics and, 72-73
  by Jewel, 55, 74-75
  soul leadership, 34-35
  spirituality and, xiv, 37, 41, 42, 79-80
  spiritually guided leadership for social justice, 72-75, 87-90
  spiritually guided leadership through servanthood, 64-67, 80-82
Leadership theory, xviii, 24, 25-28
LeCompte, M.D., 45
Lemert, C., 17, 18
LLS, 17
Lorde, A., 63

M

M Street High School for Colored Youth, 18
MacGregor Burns, J., 82
Marable, M., 5-6
Mary, Mary, 8
Mbiti, 24
McKay, N., 12-13
Mentoring
  by Adjuoa, 83
  by Chaka, 84, 86
  by Jewel, 86-87
Miami University, violence in, 88
Miller, N., 7
Miner, M., 11
Missionary philanthropy, 12
Morality, education and, 11
Morgan, G., 24, 26-27, 28
Mossell, G.B., 23
Moten, L., 13
Mullings, L., 5-6
Multivoclivity, 40
Munro, P., 7, 38-39
Murray, P., 30
Murtadha, K., 42, 88
Murtadha-Watts, K., 79, 94

N

Napier, L.A., 73, 80

National Association of College Women (NACW), 14-15
National Association of Colored Women, 20
National Association of Women Deans, 15
National Council of Negro Women, 15, 20
National Youth Administration, 21
National Youth Advisory, 21
Neumann, A., 24, 27, 28
"Nommo", 9, 94

O

"Othermothering", 83-86

P

Palmer, P.J., xii, 31, 32, 72, 87
Paris, P.J., 24, 31-32, 82
Peake, M., 10
Perkins, L.M., 15-16
Philanthropic foundations, 12
Preissle, J., 45
Prince, M., 9-10
Prophetic pessimism, 97-98

Q

Quantz, R., 28-29, 42
Quinn, R., 32-33, 83

R

"Race women", 76
Racism, dealing with, 73-74
Rasor, S., 5, 31
Reid-Merritt, P., 25
Religion. *See* Black church; Spirituality
Research methodology, 35-46
  data and analysis, 42, 45-46
  interview participants' stories, 48-61
  interview process, 42, 43-45, 104
  participants, letter to, 103-105
  participants, selecting, 43
  research design, 44-45
Research participants
  interview process, 42, 43-45
  selection of, 43
  See also Adjuoa; Chaka; Jewel
Rogers, J., 34
Royster, J.J., xviii

S

Sanchez, S., 8
School violence, 87
Schools, 10-11
Scotia Academy, 11
Seidman, I., 42, 44-45, 46
Servanthood, spiritually guided leadership through, 64-67, 80-82
Sexism, dealing with, 73-74
Simmons, R.J., 25
Slowe, L.D., 13-17, 21, 76
Smitherman, G., xvii
Social justice, spiritually guided leadership for, 72-75, 87-90
Sojourner Truth, 8, 53
Soul leadership, 34-35
Sounds of Blackness, 8
Spelman College, 11
Spiritual leadership, 37, 98
  See also Spiritually guided leadership
Spiritual theory, xviii, 24, 31-35
Spirituality, 3-4, 7, 31-32
  Adjuoa's story, 51
  Black church, 11-12, 58, 96
  Chaka's story, 58-59, 96
  definitions of, 4-5
  Jewel's story, 55-57
  leadership and, xiv, 37, 41, 42, 79-80
  Stewart on, 98

Spiritually guided leadership
of Adjuoa, 64-65, 80, 89
of Chaka, 66-67, 80, 89
of Jewel, 65-66, 80, 89
for social justice, 72-75, 87-90
through servanthood, 64-67, 80-82
Spirituals, 5-6, 7-8
Springer, K., 91-92
Stake, R.E., 37
Starratt, R.J., xii, 26, 28, 93
Stewart, C.F., 4-5, 7, 24, 31, 92, 98
Story-telling, xvi

T

Teaching, 11, 51-52
Terrell, M.C., 13
Thompson, K., 11
Thompson, L., 39-40
Traditional dress, 49
Triple consciousness, 98
Tuskegee Institute, 11

V

Violence in schools, 87

W

Wa Thiong'O, N., 88
Walker, A., 30
Washington, D.E., 98
Washington, M., 13
Washington Preparatory High School for Colored Youth, 18
Welch, 24, 31
Wells-Barnett, I.B., 20
West, C., 7, 24, 97
Wheatley, 24, 31
White, A.M., 93
Wilson, E.J., 19
Womanist theory. *See* Feminist/womanist theory

For Product Safety Concerns and Information please contact our EU representative GPSR@taylorandfrancis.com Taylor & Francis Verlag GmbH, Kaufingerstraße 24, 80331 München, Germany

Printed and bound by CPI Group (UK) Ltd, Croydon, CR0 4YY

08/06/2025

01896982-0002